FUNG SHWAY

How to Apply the Ancient Principles of Feng Shui to A Modern Day Lifestyle

By Jus One

Printed in the United States of America
First Printing, 2017
ISBN 0998389323
HDB Publishing LLC
www.HdbPublishing.com
First Edition

HDB

P U B L I S H I N G

For Alym - "Your super power is being you!" Daddo

Table of Contents

Introduction

First of all, I think it's extremely important to mention the best way to read this book is with an open mind. The emphasis should be placed on the word "open" before we continue. This book is meant to serve as a gateway into allowing new and inspiring situations into your life. The key to adding anything into your life is having the space for it. We all must learn how to delegate space in the correct ways to welcome new things into our lives. Far too often do we allow clutter to invade our space literally as well as figuratively. What does this mean? It means the clutter becomes binding, leaving us drained, tied down, and often confounded unbeknownst to our present mind. The clutter we see around us daily is a direct result of the mindset we employ, whether we choose to acknowledge it or not. For example, when we are in a messy room and decide to straighten it up, the act of cleaning it up comes from the mind's desire to organize. If we choose not to clean up and find comfort in the mess, it is the mind's desire to be in chaos, and the body will follow accordingly. The room that you are in becomes an outward manifestation of the mental state that you are in. In plain words, a messy room is the result of a messy mind. Your mind and your life are just as messy as the room you are in.

The focus of this book is to aid you in restructuring your mind, to restructure your environment, which will in turn restructure your life, with you at the helm donning the position of the architect. This truly is about renovating the mind. There are many publications on this topic, some very useful and some not so much, but this one will be tailored to applying these principles in areas and situations that often require a special skill set to achieve the desired goal. Most authors that decide to speak on this topic often evade the application of these principles in certain environments. Although I highly doubt that it's being done maliciously, the fact remains that there has been a serious void left in explaining these principles where they are sometimes needed the most. Simply put, when thinking of acquiring a Zen-like peace, cities like Chicago, New York, Philadelphia, or L.A., aren't exactly ideal representations of such, but could greatly benefit from these principles if explained how they can directly apply to the busy lifestyles of its occupants. With that being said, I'd like to assume the position of your tour guide into a new world of possibilities that can only come from within, by giving you the keys to unlocking your mind and unleashing your potential onto the world.

No stone in this rock garden will be left unturned as we uncover the true roots to achieving and sustaining a quality life. We will aggressively decipher the manner in which we handle very difficult situations in even more difficult environments, while also focusing on the different types of individuals that will be attempting to do so. Can peace, tranquility, and mastery exist in the modern day dynamic that we currently face? The answer for me is absolutely and in the confines of these pages, you will discover why it's so easy for me to say so. With all that being said, I ask you, "Are you ready to embark on a journey within?" In full disclosure, I'd like let you know that we are still at the gate and its not too late to close this book and turn back, but for those of you ready to embrace the potential you have within it is now time to buckle up, the ride is beginning shortly.

Meet Your Tour Guide

Normally I find introducing myself to be a much simpler concept, but in this regard I'm sure it will prove to be a slightly more difficult task than before. Some sound advice that I've learned along my way has always been to take advice from the experts. Meaning, if you're going to learn how to play basketball, don't consult the football coach. Keeping that principle in mind, I think it's only fair to acknowledge that I'm probably the furthest thing from a monk that you will find, yet as I've mentioned before, this book pertains to applying the monk-like qualities in an area where it seems nearly impossible to do so. Using the same basketball analogy, Michael Jordan is considerably the best player of all time, with an undeniable combination of talent and skill. However, this doesn't mean that he can come into the streets and shoot at the same percentage while aiming at a milk crate nailed to a telephone pole? Although he is a great player, when playing the game in an unfamiliar setting, the environment dictates a different application of his skills. Adjustments must be made in order to achieve the same results he would receive if playing on a court. He would have to have the correct presence of mind to adapt to the conditions surrounding him in order for his talents to flourish. Again, I am no monk, nor am I Michael Jordan, but in terms of applying the principles of this ancient art in these modern times, I'm fifty four fifty while shooting at the crate! Those of you who've read my previous publication know that I'm no stranger to the city life, but for those of you that haven't this book will certainly give you an understanding of who I am but more importantly you will discover more about yourself and that is the intention of this book.

The truth of the matter is that who I am is of no consequence. What this publication is about is discovering who you are by equipping yourself with the proper tools to do so. This is not about a bunch of feel good rhetoric or accidentally stumbling into the true nature of yourself. This about using the necessary tools to properly unearth what lies beneath bettering ourselves in the process. My concern is that the confines of this book teach you more about yourself rather than using this as a way to glorify myself. It's now time for the opening of the first chapter, which will be the breaking of the seal that keeps our minds closed off from the hidden potentials waiting to be unleashed. Let's begin.

Chapter One
The Art of Preparation

What is Feng Shui? Well, to describe this 3,000 year old principle in its simplest form, Feng means water and Shui means wind. Of the five elements that compose this ancient art, these two represent the flow of energy. Within this science, wind and water are heavily associated with good fortune and positive energy. This energy may consist of healthy relationships, wealth, positive interactions, and an overall positive outlook on life as a whole. Understanding these principles and infusing them in our daily lives will not only help the flow of positivity to find its way into our surroundings, but find comfort by the acceptance of it. The art of Feng Shui focuses on the placement of key elements in specific positions to allow this positive energy to flow. This book focuses on the mental application of this principle teaching us how to organize our thoughts and actions to allow our physical bodies to create positive manifestations of the energy that flows through us. After all, we are what we are and the magnitude of this phrase will unfold as these pages are turned.

People often question how things derived in ancient times hold relevance today. The truth is that the principles that were developed in these times of antiquity hold more relevance now than ever before. When things evolve, they tend to convolute the initial intentions that were conceived at the core. As man continues to build we stray further away from the principles of life created in the moments of clarity formed by life's simplicity. It was these principles that activated the potential in man to begin building in the first place. However, with more external construction began the destruction of self. This is the nature of the universe. Two things cannot occupy the same space at the same time. By acknowledging this, we will be temporarily taking the focus off of what we as modern humans have built and focusing on what we've destroyed.

This book has been carefully crafted to unlock our latent potential and activate the better side of yourself. This in not about giving you power, it's designed to help you access the power you already posses. We all have abilities that are harnessed but certainly underutilized. In no way should this publication be misconstrued as a fluffy, feel good placebo for the real issues in life that ail us. This is the breaking down and reconstruction of the self that we know. Pay close attention to the principles and practices laid out for you as you embark on this unique journey into the center of yourself. Now without further delay, let's begin.

The Truth About Attraction

We've recently seen an explosion in the acknowledgment of what's known as the law of attraction. This discovery by many serves them well and avails them to other principles that they may not have been aware of previously. The study of this principle in itself attracts positive energy, because most people that seek this information are not looking to attract negative energy to themselves. The problem lies in the description of the principle and the lack of control that it evokes. It's description sounds a lot like magic and magic relies on an illusion. What tends to happen is people assume that being positive and keeping a positive mind frame will attract positivity in their lives and end up waiting for these great things they're attracting to manifest in their lives before their eyes. The problem with this type of thinking is it relies far too much on waiting. During this waiting process a new energy will begin to set in. It's the equivalent of waiting in a line for something that you want or need without seeing movement in the line. This scenario leads to a mounting frustration level that will progress into anger and it is that anger that is the breeding ground for negative energy. Is it truly possible for us to mentally attract physical things without physical activity? The answer is, absolutely. However, relying on this is not a rational ideal to invest in. It is absolutely true that you can walk around with positive spirits that rub off on others and may result in someone giving you an extra scoop of ice cream at the parlor, but it you are tightly clenching a lottery ticket in your hand, thinking that you've been positive all week and surely your reward will be announced on the evening news, you are setting yourself up for grave disappointment.

The truth is that energy cannot be destroyed, only the charge of the energy can change. For instance, when we try to purposely evoke the power of attraction we may initially set out with positive energy that eventually transforms into negative energy out of frustration. The problem lies when we attempt to rationalize what we don't understand. This would create confusion for anyone in any arena in life. Imagine a lawyer that jumps into a courtroom to defend a client in a case that they have no knowledge of. They would be rationalizing events that would be extremely difficult to defend without the luxury of information. In many cases attraction is described in a mystical sense where people are being told that they can have anything they want and often this is the only thing that resonates. There are several things that coincide with the law of attraction and having it work for you. The truth of the matter is that it takes much more to change your overall charge than simply having positive thoughts. While these thoughts are certainly pivotal in the progression of our overall being, they first have to be genuine. Walking around smiling and being overly polite in order to receive the gifts the universe was asked for is being disingenuous which has an undertone of negativity. It's the equivalent to being nice to someone only for the reason of getting something from them. People who behave this way are not generally deemed as positive people. In order to attract the things we want in our lives, we must change the charge that we project outward without compensation. Ask yourself, is the healthcare worker that helps an old woman across the street viewed in the same light as the random citizen that does the very same act? The difference is that when something is done with compensation it changes the dynamic of the situation. This doesn't mean that the healthcare worker in this scenario is solely doing this for compensation, however, the motive does matter. After all, are we trying to bring positivity to the world or just to our lives? While it is in human nature to selfishly answer this question by prioritizing the lives of ourselves and those closest to us, caring for others is what greatly contributes to calibrating ourselves positively and this is what effects our overall charge.

Opening Your Mind

Many of us believe that we are open minded and have the ability to look at things objectively until we are confronted by views and opinions that conflict with their own. The reason this particular segment is titled "Opening Your Mind" as opposed to "Have an Open Mind" is because having an open mind is the destination and opening the mind is the course. We must be able to discern between the two. In order to achieve the results we desire we have to respect the process. If you are looking for a magical solution to the problems that ail you this book is simply not for you. I'm of the mindset of easy come, easy go. When happiness is achieved by receiving something it can be taken away with the loss of that object. This is the difference between saying someone makes you happier rather than saying that you are happy when your with them. Some of you may be thinking to yourselves, "hey, as long as you're happy..." but this is what prevents you from maintaining your happiness. Let's take an in depth look at the process of opening your mind as well as keeping it open. This makes it easier to receive what the universe has to offer us, so without further ado, lets dive right into the process and see if we can crack our minds wide open to cast a much broader net to not only capture our desires but also better understand the world we exist in.

The first thing we have to do is recognize that opening our minds is a part of a journey. However, this is not an outward journey. This is a journey within. During the course of this book we will all endure a unique process of introspection. To be clear, that's actually the purpose. While traveling its important to keep your eyes on the road and this road happens to be directing you inward. This isn't about changing yourself as much as it is about acknowledging yourself. Remember this is about process and processes do take time. The good part is that you've already started. This journey begins the moment you've decided it was necessary and all journeys no matter what the size begin with a single step. Before we get too far down the road I think the wisest thing for us to do is chart are course so that we can better understand where it is we are going. After recognizing that charting our course is the most sensible action, it's important that we don't skip a step. For the purpose of being completely thorough we must first recognize and acknowledge where we are at this point in time. The step in getting where you want to be is pointing yourself in the right direction and this can only be accomplished if you understand where you are.

Understanding Space

What's the purpose of mentioning space? Due to being wrapped up in the constraints of our daily existence many of us tend to forget the fact that we are currently suspended in space. That's right, at this very moment we are physically traveling through the universe. For some reason we often choose to either mystify or simplify our existence on this planet and in this universe. On one hand, mentioning that we are in space and are working in accord with extraterrestrial elements such as the sun, moon, and the polarities they cause will lead to being referred to as a space cadet that is completely out of their mind. On the other hand, there are those that oversimplify their existence by thinking that they are simply a human bound to the ground without the ability to comprehend their own existence. The problem with the latter situation is that you are not fully embracing your existence. The first scenario allows you to acknowledge your existence, but only if you are brave enough think outside of the box, or in this case outside of the planet. Let's begin by acknowledging where and what we are by starting off with the where.

*Where: The fact of the matter is that we are indeed on the planet earth for everyone wondering where exactly I'm going with this, but to fully comprehend the fact that we are in space and connected to the happenings of space I'll go into a bit more detail. Most of us recognize our earthly existence, but completely negate our universal existence. The fact that we know whether it is daytime or night time is a reflection of our universal understanding. We use the sun and the moon, (neither of which are on earth) to determine what time it is on our planet. In fact anyone who thinks this conversation is a little "spaced out" should never be seen with sun block while enjoying a day on the beach because the very sun that they are attempting to block is outside of this planet while emitting rays that enter the atmosphere of our planet and affect our lives. So, let's ask the question again, is it necessary to acknowledge our universal existence? Are we affected by extraterrestrial activity? Well, I think the answer is unequivocally yes. This is the beginning of expanding the way we think and also opening the mind by beginning to understand truly how big it is.

Speaking about the sun is the perfect way to discuss the nature of light. Light does travel. The light that we see from the sun is not as children would refer to as a light in the sky, because the sun is not in the sky. Some of us aren't able to see three blocks away and believe that we are able to see something that exist ninety-three million miles away. One thing about humans is we are certainly conceited beings when we choose to ignore facts. The truth is our vision isn't traveling ninety-three million miles. The light is actually traveling to us. That's correct something outside of the planet can exist on the planet effect the planet to the point of impact. Don't believe me? Go lay out in the sun for a few hours and then we'll reconvene to see if your thoughts have changed. Now that we've acknowledged somewhat of the where let's continue along to something equally as interesting, the what.

*What: The question of what we are is a little trickier to answer than the question of where we are. However, it can be answered. What we have to understand is thought. Thought is the most important aspect of what we are because it gives an indication of how our brains actually work. The key is to understand that our thoughts don't come from our brains. The brain is actually used to process and store thoughts rather than produce them. It is very similar to any other machine in that regard. Machines don't program themselves in any regard. Don't be confused by actions like muscle memory and doing things without focus and think that the brain is doing these things for you. In order to understand what we are, we have to separate the functions of the brain from the mind. There is no part of your brain that is called the mind. It is just referred to in that way because of the close relationship to it. How many times have you been in traffic and cursed at the car in front of you? Most of us will answer many times without noticing that we were cursing at the driver and not the car. This is the same close association attributed to the brain and the mind. The brain works in the same fashion that the car does, with the mind acting as the brain's driver. This book is intended to focus on the driver rather than the vehicle. So to answer the question of what we are, we are physical computers and the actions perpetrated by us are the actions of the programmer.

With the understanding that our mind is what drives the vehicle known as our bodies lets look back to the sun rays that come from outside of the planet that are felt on earth. Our thoughts work in the same cosmic way that the sun rays do. Thought travel in the same way that light does. The mind tells the brain what to do by way of sensors that respond to light. This is the reason why every thought is not acted out. The brain only does what it's told to do. In this book we will learn how to process the thoughts of our mind to create more positive actions from our physical bodies. Now that we've addressed the where and the what, the remaining question is the why and that is a question that was and will be asked for all of eternity without a definitive answer. It's both reasonable and fair to speculate the answer to this question. However, it should be noted that this one particular aspect of our lives will always remain in the realm of speculation.

Charting Our Course of Travel

It was previously stated in this book that this would be a journey within. Allow me to give you your itinerary to help guide you through this process. This itinerary is what will be detailed during the course of this book and now is the time to remind you that this should be processed must be accompanied by your own unique introspection and reflection to maximize the results designed in this publication. We will be focusing on the number nine because it represents the completion that we are looking for in our lives. The number nine is the highest digit because any numbers that come after nine are a combination of the already existing digits. Let's take a look at what we will attempt to accomplish on this journey.

Step One: Recognizing and Understanding our position

Step Two: The Clean Up our lives and environments

Step Three: Creating an Oasis

Step Four: Taking care of our physical being

Step Five: Using and understanding the elements

Step Six: Building our self and our wealth

Step Seven: Strengthening our relationships

Step Eight: Becoming conscious

Step Nine: Arriving at your destination

Before proceeding I would like to share with you one of the greatest principles in the universe. This is actually the glue to it all. It is a universal understanding of all things combined. You can ponder the details of our existence at your own discretion. However, this very simple principle is an undisputed fact of everything we know and don't know all rolled into one. The principle I'm speaking of is known as The All.

The All
Nothing is a Part of Everything

Let's take a look at everything! The ability to open and expand your mind can be greatly increased by understanding the concept of ALL. There is simply nothing that can exist outside of it including the concept of nothing. The same principle applies to mathematics rendering zero a number. Once you identify it it become something. In essence, what we are saying is that nothing is something and in order to look at everything we must include nothing. Understanding this will open your mind beyond the limits of your imagination and comprehension and will also aid you in the journey of understanding yourself and where you fit in. The idea of all also represents a perfect form of balance because everything has an opposite. Without left there would be no right. Without the existence e up, there would be no down, and most importantly for this discussion, without negative there would be no positive. There is duality in all things and concepts, making the world and universe more diverse than we could possibly imagine. We exist in the balance that is created by this balance and have the ability to access both negative and positive energy at will. We have the choice to view things from whatever perspective, we like when we understand the greater principle of all. This can create a shift in our lives that most people had no idea was possible. This involves much more than looking at a glass and deciding if it is half full or half empty, however the root principle is the same. The focus should lie on our power and ability to choose. In many cases we don't have the ability to choose what happens to us in our lives, but we always possess the power of deciding how we are affected and how we choose to respond. What happens to us in our lives may simply be the result of living in a world with other living beings and crossing paths with other decision makers, but its how we respond and internalize these happenings that define our being.

Some might say people can't change, they are who they are. What they don't understand is that it isn't the person we are looking to change, it's the decisions that they make that are subject to change. At any moment the decisions we make and the way we make decisions can change. The phrase "I changed my mind" tends to stick out when discussing this topic. It's something that we've all said at one point or another, so it will be easy for us to identify with the mindset we had while uttering this phrase. Ask yourself, did you change your mind, or did your mind change you? First of all, this phrase creates a separation of things that are not separate. You changed your mind? Is your mind not you? Is your mind controlled by you, or do you control your mind? All of these concepts that are deemed separate are actually pulled together by the concept of ALL. The mind, body, spirit, and soul are all interconnected as one and are strengthened by acknowledging this fact as an undeniable truth. After realizing the connection that exist within ourselves, we an begin to connect to the people around us. This connection is a little more difficult to accomplish because of our desire to be individually unique. What we must realize is that there is simply nothing we can do to not be individuals and not be unique, so trying to do so is a futile effort. The ALL binds us together in a variety of different ways, but at the core it binds us simply because we are all a part of it. This is what connects us to any and everything in some way. Whether plant life, animal life, human beings or the earth itself, we are ALL connected. Exploring these connections is not what keeps us connected, it's what strengthens our connection to the energy that we wish to attract.

Chapter Two
The Beginning: Cleaning Up

What are the benefits of cleaning up? Besides general health concerns, there are many specific health concerns that correlate with both physical and mental health issues that can be directly affected by the level of cleanliness in our environments. We will explore the positives and negatives of clutter in our lives and the ramifications that are ascribed to such behaviors. Can the mess of another hinder our progress? What steps should be made to sidestep such a situation? Is it possible to live without any clutter at all? These questions will be more than explored in this segment, they will be definitively answered.

Cleanliness is Next to Godliness

Cleanliness is next to Godliness is much more than just a famous phrase. It is a reality that even an atheist could find value in. When looking at the attributes of what many consider to be God or at the very least Godlike, we will find creation to be the most powerful of them all. Creation is what separates your God from a superhero who may posses super strength, speed or some other ability that the average human doesn't. God has the ability to create and that is our strongest asset. When we are looking to create our environment helps to dictate what we bring into existence based off of what already exist around us. Think about entering a kitchen to bake a cake. You'll have two options for this exercise. The first is a kitchen that hadn't been cleaned in days. It has crumbs on the counter, utensils in the sink an overflowing trash can as well as a broken light bulb hanging over a sticky stove top. The second option consists of a kitchen with bright and clean stainless steal, neat and organized utensils, with bright and inviting lights shining over the stove top. I think we all can see that one environment is more conducive to display our Godlike abilities of creation in, the clean one!

When we put this into perspective, we can easily see that a clean environment is much easier to bring things into existence. When things are in their proper place it leaves room for a natural order to take place. Creation is a result of the natural order. When a seed is planted in the soil, exposed to sunlight and watered, it allows nature to take its course and creation to ensue. The same results can be achieved with something less attractive, such as mold growing on bread in a dark cabinet. The environment dictates creation. Have you ever wondered why the music that come from the ghetto is such a mixture of beauty and pain? I'm sure you haven't, because it's pretty obvious that what's being created there is a result of the surroundings its being created in. Our results often reflect our beginnings. Does this mean that everything created in a better environment comes out better than its competitors? Absolutely not! What it shows is that the chances of it being better are far greater and if you can create a masterpiece amongst destruction and turmoil, you may find your potential to be limitless in a setting that is designed to suit you better.

When looking further into the creative aspects of our lives, we'll find that it permeates most aspects of the situations around us. I'm not suggesting that there will ever be a time when we will be in complete control of every single thing that occurs in our lives, because there will always be the existence of variables. Outside influences will certainly find their way into our life situations, but the more control we have over our lives, the better equipped we are to handle these situations accordingly. Before this begins to turn into a ramble, I'll simplify things to make everything that I've come to understand understood. The cleaner our environment is, the easier it is to create. Creation is the biggest aspect of our lives because we possess the ability to create everything in our lives. We create the situations that bring good or bad energy into our lives, and knowing this should inspire us to keep a clean environment to create in.

Let's take a second to examine in detail the how cleanliness translates into better situations, and adversely how the lack of cleanliness contributes to a hindering confusion. We'll break these topics into two categories, physical and mental, to evaluate them correctly on their own platforms.

The Physical State of Cleanliness

When speaking on physical cleanliness, we all would like to consider our self clean. Although personal hygiene is a big part of physical cleanliness it is not the focus of this particular segment. I'm not here to remind you to wash in between your toes and behind your ears. I'm going to assume your bathroom rituals are up to par and simply suggest that if not you should apply a more concerted effort to do so. This is dealing with the cleanliness of our physical bodies, environments, as well as possessions.

First things first, I'd like to quickly touch on the power of confidence. Confidence often starts off as an invisible element but ends up being quite visible in the eyes of many. People often assume that confidence is solely a personality trait that we are either blessed with or simply don't have at all. What I've come to realize s that confidence comes from knowing and that is the battery of the confident people in our world. Allow me to show you a quick and easy formula for stimulating confidence. When you hear a surprise knock at your door, how comfortable are you with opening it and welcoming a guest into our life. Do you hear the knock and say let me run and put something on? Let me run and pick up these clothes on the floor, or hide this mess. If an unexpected guest was to enter, is the first thing that you have to say "Please excuse the mess"? Although a lot of the time a mess of some degree is completely understandable it can effect the level of confidence we acquire as well as exude.

Confidence exists within our levels of comfort. For example, lets look at the previous scenario and apply different levels of comfort.

A stranger (cable guy, electrician, etc.) knocks on the door and you have a mess:

Knowing that you are quite possibly never going to see someone again and having no desire to due so enables the mind to create a safety net for our comfort levels. This can in many cases lead to empty excuses and dismissal. Unfortunately for people who continue to operate this way, where the mind goes the body follows. Getting trapped in this state of being prevents future positive interactions from being formed.

A family member or friend that has seen your mess before knocks on your door:

There is an obvious sense of ease provided from the presence of a friend or family member. While in most cases, you would personally prefer to be seen in a consistent positive light, the sight of an unsightly mess wouldn't be enough to break a bond

A news reporter with a news camera knocks on the door:

This situation is unequivocally the most drastic out of all of the previous scenarios. It forces us to put our entire living situation into perspective. By presenting ourselves to the world, we automatically attempt to exhibit our best qualities in order show ourselves in the best light. If we are in a state where we feel comfortable opening the door for anyone, we are at the highest level of comfortability which translates into the confidence we need to tackle anything.

Your Physical Environment

Clarity:

When our physical environments are in the proper conditions they help to fuel our physical being in several different ways. The first and most prominent change of them all is the gift of clarity, which is by far an invaluable

Fung Shway

asset to anyone in any situation. Cleaning and maintaining a cleanly environment provides a relief that happens immediately! There is simply no wait involved before seeing the fruits of your labor. This is the kick start that many of us need in our lives to begin seeing our endeavors through and is the first step on the ladder to success. Without delving into the metaphysical realm to study how thoughts are transmitted as light which bounces off of things, we can take a look at common situations and find that depression and clutter are often linked. The moment you decide to clean your surroundings was your first moment of clarity. Simply knowing this is not enough. Only when the first step is taken is the connection made, giving you the results that can only be accomplished through action. Watching a room begin to go in order is very different from actually putting a room in order. The old phrase "where the mind goes the body will follow" is a very prevalent one in regards to this conversation. You can't begin the process without acknowledging the problem. It is in that acknowledgment that the seed for action is planted, creating the first stage of clarity. It is in the second stage of action that the immediate response is given to your efforts. The bottom line is we must create open and inviting environments in our lives to welcome positive new situations that will better our circumstances. We need to begin to personify positive situations and treat them like a wanted and respected guest by having pleasant and accommodating surroundings intended to keep them around.

Mental Cleanliness

Speaking on the importance of mental cleanliness can be a very tricky thing to do. It becomes a great balancing act because the mind is our most unique trait and asset. We may feel similar to others in many ways, yet the mind is free to roam twenty-four hours a day even while in the presence of others. Everyone has their own moral compass and their own unique idea of what should be acceptable in something as private as their own thoughts. I am in know way telling you what to think, the key lies in how you think. People often guard the right to have their own thoughts viciously and aggressively and are absolutely correct in doing so. The problem arises when we conflate this issue and don't differentiate the differences between what to think and how to think. The difference is simple methodology. For instance, in the realm of art, someone teaching you correct brush strokes and paint techniques is very different from someone standing over you telling you what to paint. The brush strokes and techniques is the methodology you will use to express yourself in any way that you choose. The same applies to our thoughts and our thought patterns. One thing no one can ever take from you is a thought and we have to remember that when leaning new processes of thinking.

We've already discussed how the clutter of your mind parallels the clutter in your physical environment, but lets take a look from the opposite perspective. Sometimes we have to modernize our thoughts, in the same way that you would modernize your home. Old ideologies can stagnate our minds from progression, very similar to old outdated furniture. This is not to say that everything old should be discarded and thrown away. It simply means that the thought of ridding this from your life should be taken into consideration. Some ideologies liken themselves to a classic piece of furniture that only a fool would throw away and find them selves being displayed and treated better than new things that haven't quite earned themselves the status of classic. In other words, some things are classics and some things are just old. In something as unique as the mind it will be up to the individual on what things or thoughts deserve to remain where they are.

One thing that I've found to be very intriguing is the concept of insanity. I'm sure people that know me personally would find this hilarious due to the fact that they would love to call me crazy, but the fact of the matter is the concept of insanity is an overlooked phenomenon that needs to be explored before attempting to organize the mind. Insanity by definition is the act of doing the same thing over and over and expecting a different result. Doing the same thing and thinking the same things can be equally detrimental when seeking certain results. This brings us back to the point of methodology and learning the correct ways to organize our thoughts. In attempts to guard our sacred rights to our own thoughts we sometimes negate the fact that our thoughts may not be our own. We have to ask ourselves, "Is this my own thought or have I been indoctrinated?".

Indoctrination can be a very sneaky and subtle process that rears its head without notice. I once had a conversation with a young women that worked a rehab facility about her interactions with her patients. She spoke to me about a comment that her patient said to her and her response sparked my interest. When speaking on how their life had lead them into drugs and later addiction, the patient said "I'm a product of my environment" and she replied "That's nonsense, I'm from the same environment". I attempted to look at each of these statements equally and asses them. I explained to her that he was absolutely correct and so was she, the confusion came from the methodology in which they were thinking.

Allow me to explain in detail before showing you how this correlates to the topic at hand.

Product of my environment: Isn't everything a product of it's environment? If you attempt to grow a palm tree in the streets of New York City, the chances of you successfully doing so is little to none. However, creating an indoor environment that is properly equipped with the right temperature and light will provide a different result. The things we see are products of their surroundings. This doesn't mean that only one outcome is possible. For instance, lets take a look at a scenario with two children living with parents that yell and curse on a consistent basis. One of these two children may continue to raise their children in a similar fashion. The other might take an extreme route not allowing any cursing in their home at all. Both of these children and their future actions are products of their environments, although they have a clear distinction in the way they choose to handle things it was the environment the seed was planted in that greatly influenced the result. When people refer to this phenomenon as nonsense they are often focusing on an anomaly or even in some cases denial. No matter how unlikely the may be, we must acknowledge the anomaly for the sake of being just and thorough.

Fung Shway

The reality of the matter is that being a product of your environment cannot be evaded, but this should in no way entail being trapped by an environment or allowing the environment to dictate your outcome. We often hear the phrase "rise above your environment", but the true meaning is to rise above the negative situations in that environment that can affect you adversely. Rising above an environment will only place you in a new environment that you will then be a product of. Your focus should be to keep the negative energy beneath you, rather than focusing on an environmental change. The gift many of us encounter is that those of us who strive to rise above negative situations end up changing the environment for the better in doing so. This is one of the universe's blessings bestowed upon the righteous. Recognizing indoctrination is key in the mental cleaning process. It is the equivalent of thinking trash and poverty go together. In some ways they do, but its the indoctrination of our thought patterns that make this true. This brings me to a point that I find extremely worth of exploration. Lets take a look at the correlations between trash and poverty and how they effect the mindset of those living in these environments.

The Intimate Relationship Between Trash & Poverty

What came first, the chicken or the egg? While some of us who haven't studied biology and even some of us that have may find this to be debatable, the answer doesn't seem to be an absolute. On the other hand, I think its safe to assume the conditions of poverty were here before the trash. I think by now we are all aware that the poorest neighborhoods can be easily spotted by the unsightly trash that is dispersed throughout its surface. This becomes a circle of events creating a trap for the residents and a repellent for those that come from other places. It also speaks in great detail about the mindset of these occupants. When living with the burden of poverty you can find yourself drained mentally as well as physically. This produces the lack of energy needed to maintain cleanliness in this environment. After reaching this point your energy becomes toxic and the environment perpetuates the toxicity in most cases leading to a negative existence. Let's for a second imagine living in a great deal of poverty and squaller and visiting a community that is full of abundance, vitality and void of visible garbage. Upon returning to your community you may feel drained as soon as arrive. Your physical surroundings are directly effecting you negatively and could quite possibly consume you in the process. Adversely, you may come home with the energy to restore your environment to its grace, but find that you are alone in this particular endeavor.

What is the remedy? The remedy is to control what you have control over in hopes that others will follow suit. This will change your environment. Most people think that a change in environment means you have to literally pack up and move away, but this is not the case. Simply cleaning your home and its surroundings creates a change in environment that can not be impeded on by poverty. Many of us are trapped in the lazy state brought on by the negativity that surrounds us. Imagine living in this type of neighborhood and instead of giving your street address you are now able to instruct people to come to the cleanest house on the street. While a statement like this doesn't have to actually be said, you have now become the most positive person on your street and are indirectly encouraging others to follow your shining example. how do you think your neighbors will feel telling others to come to the house next to the nice one? doesn't sound too appealing now does it? This is how you can change your environment for the affordable cost of nothing!

There is a scene in one my favorite movies "Coming to America" where a prince of an African country visits a destitute neighborhood in Queens NY. He is completely captivated by the garbage seen throughout the streets and says "Imagine a land so free one can throw garbage into the streets". While this statement is very true, it is also true that the very same people are also free to pick it up, rendering the trash a decision hat has been been made. This a decision to welcome negative energy into our lifestyles and can be changed simply by deciding not to. If you were standing on a street filled with trash while eating a snack would you throw the wrapper onto the pavement amongst the other trash, or would you search vigorously for a trash can? Being completely honest, I myself was previously of the mindset of "what difference does it make?" Personally, I've come to realize the power of attraction and will not do on another street what I won't do on my own. I make the clear decision to not add to the negativity plaguing the street. However, many of us do not think this way. The trash on the ground evokes the law of attraction making others feel it's appropriate to add to it, creating an unfavorable backdrop for others. I don't expect everyone to go on a crusade to rid the inner cities of trash, but what i will say is that keeping your own environment clean as well as picking up waste from other areas when possible builds a wall of positivity around you that will in turn attract more positivity in your lives.

Summary

The bottom line is that cleaning up is the first step of this journey, due to it's significance. It doesn't matter where you are physically, one thing you should always welcome into your life is positive energy. Positive energy can often manifest itself in the form of a blessing or what is simply referred to as "a good thing". It's a common belief that those who are in the worst of conditions are the ones who deserve a blessing first and foremost. However, needing a blessing and deserving one are two very different things. Using our previous example lets look at the benefit of having a home on your street that is presented using the best of your abilities. Imagine yourself as a blessing coming down your street. Sure, you may find yourself occasionally stoping by a house that is in need of a serious cleanse, but it isn't the type of place where you would want to stay a while or even visit too frequently. With this in mind you should be able to see one of the reasons why some people aren't visited often by positive and progressive forces, yet negative energy will easily hang out and make itself right at home.

This principle of cleanliness applies to every aspect of our being. Whether we're talking about our homes, cars, work place, or even our minds, the state of cleanliness gives us the time and space to master our environments rendering us the master of our environments. Now some might say you must first master yourself before mastering your environment, but this is a journey within, starting with our environment and moving inward. Its actually how we create environments that welcome opportunities into our lives that helps to influence our position in life. Having an open and inviting

Fung Shway

space only makes things easier to manage, gifting us with the presence of clarity and there's nothing like flying through clear skies!

Chapter Three
Finding & Maintaining
Your Oasis

Life In The Oasis:

W hat is an oasis? Well, one thing is for sure, we are not referring to an area of fertile soil in the middle of a desert. What we are speaking about is a place of refuge, away from the turmoil and conflicts of our inner city existences. These particular types of refuge are both found and created and require daily maintenance to remain beneficial to us while on our journeys. Having a place retreat is a marvelous as well as necessary feeling that we should have the opportunity to afford. This in some cases may also extend to a mental retreat that we can escape to even while in the midst of the chaos. In this chapter, we will explore how to find build and maintain our own individual oasis and secure it in order to better our lives with the positive energy that embody it.

The first step in this process is knowing what your oasis consists of. As individuals we all have different desires and ideas when it comes to where we would like to retreat to and what type of environment it consists of. Although along our travels we will meet others that share similar concepts and ideas, our oasis should be painted with our own brush and tailored to our individual desires. Knowing what you want sounds a lot easier that it actually is. Thoughts and feelings can change just as rapidly as the light that transmits them, making our oasis a delicate mixture of our short term feelings infused with our long term goals. This is the reason it requires a conscious effort to maintain the environments compatibility with its intended use. To begin, we will focus on how to find out what it is we are looking for in our lifestyles by examining one of our most powerful assets, our dreams.

The Power of Dreaming

Do dreams really come true? Absolutely! When we fully understand that our dreams are connected to us, we will slowly begin to realize that our dreams are us, rendering them already true. Have you ever stopped to ponder what a dream really is. The thought of it should truly amaze anyone who dares to think about how something like a dream is even possible. Examining the dictionary's definition or lack of definition gives us a glimpse into how powerful a dream actually is. It is described simply as a succession of images that play in One's mind while sleeping and can also be committed to memory. The key word in their definition is mind. Where and what exactly is this thing called the mind and how can we use it to our best advantage? Knowing that the insides of our physical bodies are filled with blood, veins, tissue, organs, and bones, it doesn't sound feasible that there would be any room in our bodies for a projection screen to display these recurring images that are so vaguely spoken on in the dictionary's definition. So how is it possible that we can close our eves and see, close our ears and hear, or even in some cases feel sensations while our physical body has shut down for the evening? The answer for me in short is quite simple, I don't know. Without studying exactly what chemicals are released in the brain causing us to hallucinate while sleeping we can still examine the powers of the mind and learn how to use them.

What I do know is that while most people feel that their dreams are an uncontrollable phenomenon that will take place with or without their participation, they are only partly correct. The dream world is directly linked to our imaginations. This is the key to unlocking our hidden potentials and even more importantly, creating our own existences. We have all experienced strange dreams where it seems that almost anything is possible, only to awaken and wonder why our minds chose to go to such a place. This is a wonderful thing because it shows us just how vast our mental landscape can extend. Here I will teach you how to use this power before you fall asleep to send you off floating on a cloud of your own desires.

No more counting sheep!

The act of counting sheep is tried and proven technique of falling asleep due to its repetition and otherwise boring nature. This is a waste of the powers that the dream state holds. The realm of our dreams should be controlled by us. Why would we spend it counting sheep? A method that I've used and found extremely successful is to create my dreams before falling asleep. I was having what was considered to be a reoccurring nightmare, which was really just an uncomfortable situation that found its way into my dreams every night. Before going to sleep one night I decided that I didn't want to have that reality anymore and decided to take action. I laced back on my pillow and decided to fill my dreams with all of the things that I wanted before drifting off. Yes, I filled my dreams with all of my desires, many of them material possessions, while in an environment of my choosing. You might be saying there is nothing spiritual about dreaming about material possessions, but that is the key. Its personal! I chose to first fill my dreams with material things because these are things that I could see in great detail. Words like health and wealth are vague terms that serve no purpose to a true dreamer or visionary. We must let go of fear and let honesty take over. After all if you can't be honest with yourself then you are in a state of denial and won't accomplish what it is you seek to accomplish because you are allowing fear to rule over honesty. Don't be afraid, harness the powers of honesty to build a dream for yourself that will fit your being like a glove.

While laying on my pillow I would first begin with my physical being. What would I like to wear in this dream? I would then dress myself in my ideal outfit, sparing no expense of course. Why would I everything is free, better I go with the top of the line. I would spend my time dressing myself from head to toe with all of the things that I liked, some things I may have already had, but that how life is isn't it? I would then move on to what I'm driving, again selecting only the best for this dream. My initial purpose was to offset the negative dreams that I was having so this one should dynamically opposite to that one. At this stage I was now dressed to perfection and in a very expensive automobile and it was time for me to pick a beautiful young lady to accompany me. Following the principle of honesty I chose to ride around with a perfect ten and felt myself slowly drifting off before completely knocking out. The next morning I felt so refreshed that I almost couldn't wait for the next evening to grab my paintbrush and create a similar masterpiece. Besides the refreshing feeling that I felt, the more important feeling was one of power. It was at this point that I realized I had the power to create my own destiny, even if only in the dream world. Just as my nightmare would sometimes enter my mind during the day, it was now replaced the dreams that i had created for myself and started to manifest physically. Where the mind goes the body will follow! I may not have acquired all of the expensive trinkets that laced my dreams, but did acquire similar things adjacent to the level that I was on. What stuck out the most to me was the fact that I experienced the same sensation in the physical world that I felt from my custom designed dreams.

What I want you to take from this section is the power of self. I don't expect you to have the same desires that I have. Maybe expensive watches and cars don't float your boat, the great thing about this exercise is they don't have to. This is completely about you. The important thing to do is be honest without limitations. This is a world where anything is possible. The phrase "The sky is the limit" doesn't apply here. If you want to get on a Volkswagen spaceship and explore the galaxy that completely up to you. The point is to think about whatever it is you desire and spare no expense on the details. If you want to travel, go there. Start your dream in another city or even country. Remove all limitations and dream big. This is how you can begin to control your narrative without going to sleep wondering where you will take yourself. You will be the creator of your own reality and that is the most powerful position that you could be in, or if you choose to, you can always count sheep!

The personal aspects of your oasis must be created with a level of enthusiasm that can only come from the real you. This is the purpose of creating its blueprint in the dream state. It allows you to honestly tap into your ideal situations in a realm of endless possibilities. The thoughts come with you when you wake up because they were made while you were awake. Your thought patterns will begin to form around the realm of possibility rather stagnate in the circumference of chance. With this newly discovered ability our decision making process will also begin to infuse with the thoughts created in our dream state. This is how we build the oasis of our dreams in the physical world. The daily maintenance your oasis demands has a lot to do with the energy allowed inside of it. This in large part deals with the type of people we allow into our sacred spaces as well as those who invade them. The energy we absorb greatly contributes to the formation of our environments and can effect its construction both negatively and positively. Let's take a look at how this occurrence in detain to gain a better understanding of what it entails.

Talking to Trees

There is an absolute value in placing plants into your home and work environments. Besides freshening the air and providing oxygen into the atmosphere the plants bring otherwise dead environments to life. The mere sight of plants in a home or workplace gives an inference of a clean and serene setting. With this being the case, the sight of plants that are in poor conditions is also an indication that the environment is not in its best capacity. Plants that are dying and are not well taken care of shows how life is valued by the owner. It can pinpoint a lack of focus or otherwise a complete disregard for the lives of others around us. Adding plants to our homes might seem like a very simple concept but I'd like to explore it in a different light.

There are many conclusive studies on the benefits of talking to your plants or playing soft music for them in enclosed environments. With that fact being fully acknowledged lets take a second to think about the trees that grow in an inner city environment. What conversations do the hear? What type of music do they endure? Are they receiving the type of positive energy needed to reciprocate positive energy back to the community. The answer is most likely no. Think about the conversations we keep as well as the people we keep them with. How do they effect the positive fields of the sanctuaries we create? Well, the answer is very simple. If positive conversations greatly improve the growth cycles of plants in our environments, then the opposite should be equally true. The plants could quite possibly be in a state of utter misery when trapped in an environment that is not conducive to their positive growth. The same can be said for us as human beings. We too require the very same positive energy to grow. For our ideas and endeavors to grow into fruition and flourish like a beautiful garden they need nurturing. No, this doesn't mean that we have to run from conversations that are at times confrontational, it means that we have to monitor these types of conversations make sure that we are not letting them invade our oasis. Lets take a look at the role different types of conversations play on the construction or destruction of our desired surroundings.

Conversations

We all have ambitions in life and desire certain specific outcomes from what we invest our time in. When you begin to sail in a desired direction, the conversations of others can become the current for our ships to sail. Positive messages can push you towards your goal, while negative ones will have you sailing against the current. Sometimes presumably negative dialogue can actually be helpful to you because it gives you the opportunity to reaffirm what it is you believe in. It works as an opposing piece of steel for you to sharpen your blade against. However, constant opposition will begin to drain you of the positive force you need to prosper. Placing yourself amongst conversations that repel your drive can be exhausting after prolonged periods of time. The conversations we engage in as well as the ones we hear become the backdrop and in some cases the soundtrack to our lives. We have to provide a concerted effort place ourselves in environments that support our visions, even if indirectly.

We should all bare witness to the powers of speaking things into existence. Try your best to engage in conversations with those that share information. You should not desire to be around those that only listen to your ambitions and desires and seek those that also have ambitions and desires that are equal in size. When speaking about your goals, people who are intimidated by them can project their negativity towards you creating a deterrent for you to see your visions come into fruition. When your excited about something those around you should also be excited. Without sharing the passion for what it is your excited about, they should be excited at your passion. When speaking on what you want you have decided to share your passion and positive energy with those around you and should be reciprocated.

Some of the world's greatest ideas and concepts are born out of conversation. Make sure that you control trivial conversations from dictating your direction. There are several different types of energy associated with conversation. Let's take a brief look at a few scenarios that we all have found ourselves in at one point or another.

Eavesdropping: We've all done it and we've all had it done to us. It's a very natural occurrence that happens quite often and is in many cases unavoidable. Eavesdropping happens regardless of the quality of the conversation, yet its the quality of conversation that suggest to us what type of filter we use when thrusted into these situations. For instance, when attempting to focus on project we have to be careful of the settings we place ourselves in due to the conversations that form around us. This is the reason why so much work is completed in coffee shops and libraries rather than street corners an other chaotic atmospheres. When in a coffee shop amongst other people attempting to do work you will often over hear many conversations, however, many of them are work related. Overhearing others working and seeking progress can be very motivational as well as informative in some cases. Placing yourself among progressive people can benefit you in a variety of ways. Adversely, non progressive environments produce just that, no progression. You often hear conversations that are of no use to you and in many cases would rather have not heard at all. We all know that when we speak in public the chances of others eavesdropping in on our conversations are very high.

Think about what information they would receive from listening in on you. Is your conversation at all progressive? What can be gained from this? Chances are if there is absolutely nothing that can be gained by others, there is not much that can be gained by you either. To advance your level of conversation you have to place yourself around progression. What purpose would it serve to hear people speaking all day and be able to take nothing that could advance you in any way. When this happens, whether you realize it or not the opposite is taking place. Instead of advancing yourself, you are hindering yourself. This is why some people would much rather read the daily paper than engage in conversations with non progressive people. Information is power and too many conversations that lack information can become your kryptonite.

Opposition: There are certain types of people that are in complete opposition to our ideologies. These people can often put us in positions where we disagree with almost everything they say and in some cases we might be that person to someone else. These particular conversations can become extremely draining and in some instances dangerous. Opposition takes work and this work becomes tiresome. Because this is the type of work that is of no benefit it is often avoided. When you find yourself repeatedly involved in these conversations out of fatigue you will begin to bottle your true feelings possibly causing a future explosion. It's better to make your feelings known to avoid the explosion and also the implosion. Disagreeing is healthy, but only in moderation. Excessive opposition stifles creativity by draining your creative forces. These oppositions reveal themselves when others present their own opinions as facts. This should serve as an extreme red flag for someone seeking to build. The counter for this is honesty. Do your best to avoid conversations where you are verbally appeasing people while mentally saying "yeah yeah yeah".

Soundboards: Soundboards can serve as a very useful tool. These are people that are very close to us in our personal lives that allow us to think out loud. Whether we are in certain creative modes or just in the mood to share our feelings, these people are there to simply let us vent. To be clear, I'm not suggesting that we should have people that are only useful as a sound board. What I am saying is that not all of our friendships work in the same capacity. Some friends allow us to vent and project in ways that others don't. We shouldn't expect everyone in our lives to function in the same ways either, but at times we all need some who will allow us to project while remaining nonjudgmental.

It is very important for me to mention when speaking about people and defining them as a soundboard not to completely objectify them. The reality is that while being described as a soundboard, the fact of the matter is they are not. Soundboards don't talk! We can't expect nor should we want a soundboard that never speaks back. While it is healthy to sometimes be able to freely speak your mind in what is known as a vent. It's unhealthy to express ideas with someone giving you the equivalent of talking to the wall. We as living beings require reciprocation when throwing ideas or feelings into the atmosphere. Speaking to people who are completely uninterested in our thoughts can in some way invalidate our being. Remember, when referring to these people as a soundboard in the analogy, it is merely a figure of speech. Don't expect those around you to encompass all the attributes of one. If that's what your looking for you can buy one. They're actually quite inexpensive.

Debate vs Argument: This section could also be titled Mental Exercise vs Mental Anguish. There is absolutely nothing wrong with a healthy debate. They actually stimulate thought and are a healthy function of the mind. The difference between the two lies in the intention. When entering a debate the intention should be to remain objective. It should be an exchange of opposing ideas and concepts while looking to come to a rational conclusion or resolve. An argument on the other hand lacks objectivity. You have entered the conversation with the feeling that you are right and the other is wrong and are attempting to force your point of view into the mind of someone else. This is the reason many of us are completely exhausted after a heated argument. Trying to force a thought into someone's head can be similar to a toddler trying to jam the square peg into the space designated for the circle peg. This toy is designed to not only teach the children shapes, its there to teach reasoning. A lack of objectivity creates a lack of reasoning and this creates arguments.

When entering a debate you should be mentally prepared to be proven wrong. This is what makes debating healthy, the fact that it leads to resolve. One phrase that seems to always get under my skin is "I don't want to argue". This particular phrase is an extremely annoying one because my reply is always the same, "then don't". It's actually that simple. Some contentious dialogue can be easily avoided by the presence of objectivity. Remember, when engaging into the types of conversations realizing that presenting an argument is different than actually arguing will serve you justly.

Small Talk: Small talk is exactly what it sounds like. It is a useful exercise when in its proper setting. When trying to be goal oriented this can potentially hinder your progress. Speaking about large concepts and goals only to be met with small or frivolous replies can also be draining to your spirit. Small talk in the case of being cordial is a very positive thing. It can lead to a larger conversation that may prove itself fruitful for you. The conflict comes with friends and associates that are only capable of this type of dialogue. What would life be without small talk? The answer is quiet. There is a definite power in silence. However, too much of it leads to monotony and in this monotony dreams and ambitions are unable to be nurtured into fruition. The key is in the balance. There is nothing wrong with some good old chit chat, in fact some of the most positive people you will encounter in life are those that can't shut up!

Music

Similar to the conversations we hold, music can have the same effects on our oasis depending on the roll we allow it to play. I'm not going to attempt to tell you what type of music you be listening to because we all have our own distinct set of taste buds when it comes to music. What I will say is that variety is the spice of life and provides a healthy amount of options for us to choose music tat suits different scenarios in our lives. Balance is the key to ensuring that we do not overdose from the influences of music. This can happen with any form of music from classical to hip hop. Broadening your musical spectrum allows you to experience more from life by exposing you to other lifestyles. Think about a bar that you have never stepped inside simply due to the music you heard coming from inside. What types of people did you miss out on meeting. This is not to be confused with being around music that doesn't resonate with your frequency. It's more about avoiding the redundancy of only knowing what you know. Think about it in these terms, imagine if a culture could only eat the food designated to that particular culture. That would mean never being able to say you ate Chinese, Italian,Mexican,Jamaican etc. This is a limited range of possibility that can mentally stagnate you making it hard to think outside of the box. Try different types of music in different settings to create environments that are comfortable with the feelings you are searching for at the moment. Don't limit yourself by only exposing yourself to one style. you can find comfort i the variety and may also find opportunity just as well.

Thanking Our Oasis

There is a very powerful force in saying Thank You. Don't believe me? Take your time one day and do something special for someone. Go out of your way to create a better situation for them and present them with a gift that took you quite some time to craft. If they accept this gift from you without saying anything to you, you have just witnessed the power of Thank You. Do you think you will be inclined to do it again? Even on a smaller scale the same effect will occur. Hold a door for someone, help them carry something, although the Thank You was not you reason for doing the kind act, the absence of it is a deterrent from repeating it. This is what is being done to the universe when we don't take the time to say Thank You. We are inadvertently showing the universe a lack of appreciation for the gifts that it crafts and presents us with. An oasis is truly a wonderful gift in itself and appreciation leads to more gifts. This is another crucial aspect to the maintenance of our oasis.

Being thankful is more than just saying the words, its about fully embracing the feelings of Thanks that will inspire the universe to give you more. While using your evening hours for the construction of your dreams will surely prove beneficial, you should make an attempt to begin every day by giving thanks. This creates a positive vibration and opens the door for you to receive positivity in return. When you hold a door open for someone you can feel the difference between someone who is saying Thank You out of habit and someone that is truly appreciative of your kindness. While it is obvious which one of these outcomes will lead to a better feeling for you, it should also be reminded the feeling that not receiving one at all will bring and on that note Thank You for reading this section!

Summary

Realizing that our oasis is always around us should be a liberating fact. It should help you further understand just how important the concept actually is. The type of environment we create for ourselves determine how we feel on a daily bases and how we feel dictates how we operate. Knowing where you want to be in life and what you want out of life is empowering. It creates the confidence, drive, and stability to make your dream a reality. Your oasis is your very own customized castle that you have crafted to host your desires and shield you from the chaos the world has to offer. Treat it accordingly and remember the power of Thanks as you explore what this beautiful life has to offer.

Chapter Four
Physical & Mental Fitness

What does it take to be physically and mentally fit? It's funny how very similar these two concepts actually are. Proper diet and the right amount of exercise can contribute greatly to the condition of our physical and mental state. Our well being should be looked at in great detail rather than shrugged off for reasons that aren't sufficient enough to hold water. Let's be honest, there is an entire industry dedicated to weight loss and fitness. Many of them are completely legitimate and well deserving of the credentials that they've acquired. However, there are also a lot that are seeking to play off of your emotions and desires rather than what really works. In order to begin with a fair playing field we must remove the falsehoods of what is fit and unfit. This book is designed to properly equip you by giving you real tools that will actually work, but that has to be a joint effort. We cannot achieve this by being dishonest about our true level of fitness. Physical and mental fitness require maintenance and upkeep to ensure that we are operating at our highest possible capacity. Knowing and understanding that none of us are perfect should not be used to shake off the responsibility of maintaining proper fitness levels. What we should remember is that the responsibility of caring for our mental wellness is solely our own. No one should be blamed for your personal wellness whether physical or mental. In this chapter, we will learn the configuration to a healthy lifestyle by exploring all of the avenues that will lead you there. Let's begin by uncovering the reason for fitness and extracting the power of purpose, which can be an immeasurable force to be reckoned with.

The Guard Must Be Fit

What's the purpose of mentioning a guard? Well, once you've properly constructed your oasis it will be a full time job guarding it. The guard must be in the right physical and mental condition to do this job adequately to ensure that there will be no breaches of the your oasis's confines. A sloppy guard will surely invite an overt invasion or even a more subtle Trojan horse style of approach to moving in on what you have taken your time to build. The physical aspects of guarding your oasis isn't about being strong enough to remove people from your environment. It deals more with your self esteem, which is an extremely important aspect of any guard. In order to be convincing the guard themselves must be convinced, standing up firmly and straight in a way that only confidence can make possible. Our physical fitness provides the ability to be comfortable in our own skin and that is one place we should always feel right at home. We can deny ourselves the true comfort of health by ignoring the need for it as well as the need to actually be comfortable. Confidence and comfortability in a guard can be enough to deter people from attempting to invade the territory that you have laid out for yourself. Let us now take a look at what it takes to maintain proper fitness levels, both mentally and physically by separating the two to look at them in greater detail.

The Diet of Consumption

Often when the word diet is used, it is referring to putting restraints on our eating habits and eliminating certain foods from what we consume. This word ironically can be used to describe everything that we consume, whether good or bad. Our bodies have what's known as a digestive system that is used to process the foods we eat and our minds have an equivalent to this process as well. What we eat can have a direct effect on our physical and mental state, but this is about much more than eating, it's about consumption. We consume negative and positive foods as well as negative and positive thoughts. What we consume daily contributes to how we operate daily and this is another aspect of our lives that requires attention.

Whether we choose to act on it or not is one thing, but I'm sure most rational people will agree that natural lifestyles lead to much healthier living than other lifestyle choices do. Foods that come directly from nature have a more positive impact on our bodies and are much more easily digested. Processed foods can contribute to our stagnation by not providing us with the right fuel to energize our action. Foods are supposed to sustain our bodies by providing nutrients that nurture our productivity. This is not a coincidence that these words are so similar. Nature, nurture and nutrient all belong to the same family. Lets be honest, the body stores food and processes food, so we have to look directly at consumption to avoid processing junk. Ive broken this section into parts for the purpose of being thorough to gain a clear understanding of the concepts being presented.

You Are What You Eat!
Physical Consumption

Natural: Following the model of pros vs cons we will begin with the pros which lands us directly in the natural food section. There are many forms of healthy eating depending on your commitment to your body. Unhealthy lifestyles make the right choices much more clear, yet much harder to engage in. The wrong choice have led us directly into physical addiction to sugars and other processing agents that have infiltrated our systems making it a more difficult task to make decisions based on health rather than taste. This doesn't mean I'm going to feed the myth of healthy foods not tasting good. What it does mean is that I'm going to identify the problem at its source and that myth is at the root of it.

It's now time to ask a dangerous question, women strap on your seat belts. Are you happy with your body? Are there changes you wish you could make to your body immediately? The answer for most non health orientated people will most likely be yes. Well, my next question would be what are you doing about it, or have you chosen to ignore it? Making changes in our lives is far from an easy thing to do, yet like the other things we've discussed in this book and things to come, it all begins with the acknowledgement. Even if we acknowledge that we have a problem that we have no idea how to fix, the process has begun and success is in the achievement of answering our problems. A journey of a thousand miles begins with one step and taking a step towards fitness is the same as any other journey. Lets begin this journey by looking at some healthier options for us and examining some of the benefits that come from them.

Jus One

Vegan or Vegetarian? These are the top two healthiest diet choices we can make. These particular choices have made their way to this discussion by their obvious health benefits as well as the discipline that they display. The discipline aspect is partly myth because in order to see these lifestyle choices as disciplines you would first have to believe that people who participate in them are actually tempted by the junk foods that surround these options in the store. That's right we would have to believe that these people are tempted by being overweight and possibly feeling unattractive while doing damage to their system by trying to process foods that are only considered food by a far stretch of the imagination. After acknowledging and establishing a care for your body and personal health the gummy bear becomes less appealing as the walnut when choosing a topping. This not only results in becoming a healthier individual, but it promotes responsibility and that's what's required for the general maintenance of our vessels. What many health conscious individuals have figured out and seems to elude the minds of those that aren't, is that they are not tempted by taste, its the addiction to sugar that is calling them. If I was going to create a candy that was simply based on taste like most candies are, advertising no nutritional value, I would make sure that I am creating a flavorful treat full of everything needed to make you fall in love with and by all means come back for more. What many of us fail to realize is that nature has already provided us with thee options. Fruits such as kiwi, strawberries, lime and countless others have been duplicated in much unhealthier options and with less benefits for the body as well. There are plenty of options that are pleasing to the taste bud while fueling you up in the process.

Fung Shway

Start by exploring some new foods that are healthier for you. This alone will introduce you to positive environments with progressive people. Those that concern themselves with their health tend to be more open minded helping them to think outside of certain boxes. Healthier is happier! This is not a myth. Feeling tired leads to depression which takes the time that you should be enjoying life with and transforms it into a monotonous routine holding you down like the weight your putting on. We have to free ourselves from excess in order to add positivity, similar to the cleaning process discussed earlier. The fact of the matter is that are certain foods that create fuel and others that create excess. Learning proper nutrition should not be childishly shucked off with cliches of eating rabbit food. It should become a lifestyle choice because it aids you in more aspects than one. Increasing your energy levels and changing some of your destinations to more positive and progressive places is just the beginning of what healthy living can offer you. Its these changes that lead lead to far more positive situations in your life like a chain reaction, a food chain reaction. The mirror should not be your enemy. You should be excited to greet that person every morning. Remember eating makes you "feel good", but eating healthy makes you "feel good" about yourself!

Processed: Do all processed foods taste good? If not then why should all natural foods be expected to? The myth that healthy eating comes with a sacrifice of taste must be dispelled to achieve proper levels of fitness without owing crazy in the process. Just as you will not enjoy each and every type of processed food, you will also not enjoy every natural food you come across, but the search has to begin somewhere. Helping our taste buds make a natural transition can be a fun and exciting process, because it involves trying new things and exploring different options which always leads to excitement on some level. Childish diets with no nutritional value will eventually catch up to you in the long run if your lucky. The fact is for most it will most likely catch up to you a lot sooner than you'd prefer. It can sometimes be a hard thing to identify, but our energy levels and moods can be directly affected by what we eat. This fact can translate positively or negatively in regards to our relationships as well as our productivity. Sluggishness and lethargy are not exactly desirable traits among productive individuals.

People who are driven may occasional deviate from the course of healthy living, but it will always remain a staple of their personality. The phrase birds of a feather flock together definitely applies in this situation. This is the reason why we've seen the issue of weight injected into the high stakes political arena. Your weight and physical composition tells people a great deal about your personality and more specifically your commitment to responsibility.

Fast food should definitely be avoided, but only within reason. One thing that I've come to understand is that life is a mixture of emotion, responsibility and experience. We are here to experience life. This means that occasionally we will make unhealthy choices, but they are apart of our experience. However, making too many of these unhealthy choices can shorten our lifespan or limit the quality of experiences we enjoy. Overindulging in unhealthy lifestyles promotes a false sense of of happiness, or what I like to call falling in love with second place. This is what happens when we begin to pretend that we are just as happy as those who have chosen to take better care of themselves. Although I can't be certain, I have a strong suspicion that if you hand an overweight person a magic wand, one of the first things they would change is their physical appearance. This is the reality that is often avoided by those that have let their minds lead their bodies in the wrong direction. Earlier in this book I described our physical environments as a direct reflection of our mental state, but this also applies to our physical state as well. Doing what's best and doing what's easiest are two very different things. We have to learn how to make what's best become easier than choosing other options. The key word here is "learn".

Make special note of the fact that you will rarely if ever find publications and infomercials on how to become overweight and live an unhealthy lifestyle. Their is simply no learning involved. If that's what your looking for you will easily discover the answers all around you. It doesn't take much commitment or brain power to find tasty feel good foods and this is what is displayed when we overindulge in these types of foods. It can be the equivalent to speaking to someone who has a wealth of knowledge in sports but cant speak about anything else. If your not into sports your conversations will be extremely limited or nonexistent. How will this wealth of knowledge help you in other settings where the focus is on other things such as politics and business, or even world affairs. These people will be looked at as one dimensional due to their overindulgence of one aspect of life. This is not to be confused with passion! Passion opens doors while overindulging in things locks many of the other doors that are there for the opening.

The answer to this is to find the answer. Before you throw this book down allow me to explain. When dealing with food we all have a different set of taste buds to service. The answer for me may not work for you. Exploring different options is completely up to you. The organic food industry is expanding daily with new options to make healthy living a more enjoyable experience. Don't be held down by your own ignorance, because the root of ignorance is to ignore. Just as there are fast food sources around us there a many healthier options around us as well. In the case that there aren't, this will lead you in a more positive direction forcing you in places that you haven't been before and similarly around people you haven't me before also. This is living! Making the decision to change your life for the better will send into a world of new experiences and encounters that will benefit your life in ways you have yet to imagine.

Mental Consumption

Natural: Too often our mental consumption is overlooked as something that is not as important as it actually is. We've already established the importance of diet, but our mental diet is just as important as our physical diet. Once again what lies at the root is consumption. How are minds break down and process what they take in is very impactful to the state of our mental health. in this day and age we cannot properly examine this fact without focusing on media and the role it plays in our lives. Nowadays you cant get very far without seeing someone with a phone or a tablet shoved in their face. Media has rapidly become a dominating force in our society, the question is will be let it dominate us as individuals in the same capacity. This topic is very similar to the foods we eat, knowing that eating natural and organic food is better for us we must discover how we can feed ourselves cleaner forms of media. When speaking about natural and clean forms of media it's important not to confused this with the twenty-four our watching of the nature channel. This is not what is meant by natural or clean media.

The same way we can find foods that provide nutrients necessary for our survival, we can find media that stimulates our minds in the same way. Depending on your interest there are a number of different options available for exploration that will help our minds feel energized rather than drained by the content. For instance, shows on the home and garden channel can help give us insight to different processes of building, buying and selling. You may be saying to yourself right now that you have no interest in leaning about these processes, but the positive aspect to what I'm referring to can still be found. For you it may be watching a show about the construction of a motorcycle, or something that highlights venture capitalists. Our mental taste buds are just as unique as our physical ones. The key is to try to feed our minds a healthy balance. While we all may have a number of sitcoms that we enjoy, they fall into the category of treats in the realm of media. Yes, treats are necessary to fully experience life, but they are not enough to sustain us. Overindulging in media that we cannot take anything from but a laugh is the same as living off of fast food. Different from our physical consumption clean forms of media exist all around us, and can be accessed by our fingertips. The problem is the effects are much harder to visualize. When you are consuming too much unhealthy foods the effects will manifest physically much faster than they will with the consumption of media. We have to learn how to control our mental diets in the same fashion. Thinking about the media you watch daily and how it impacts your life will help you to make better decisions on what you are willing to spend your time watching. Ask yourself, what you've learned from what you've watched and analyze what you will take from it as well.

Do you only watch things that pertain to your current lifestyle? If so, analyze your happiness level and look at the things in your life you want to change for the better. What I mean by this is if you feel that your life is full of pressure and you notice that you are only watching serious things such as the news and political shows, maybe you need n enjoyable snack and in that case its time to watch a sitcom and relieve yourself of some seriousness for a bit. Maybe you find yourself in a financial rut and are looking to escape it but your media is full of frivolousness and humor. Perhaps its time to change the channel to break up the monotony contributing to your rut. Do you live in an urban environment and only watch shows that cater to that demographic? This will not help you you to be able to expand past the borders of your environment. Sometimes we have to shock our systems by leaving our comfort zone and media that serves as comfort food. Try watching something that is completely unlike what you would normally watch and you will see how your world and appetite will expand. This will give you the fuel you need to realize that there are other worlds that exist within the one you live in leading to broader content for conversation, which will possibly land you in a better situation. At the very least you will become healthier by becoming more well rounded and versed in a variety of different topics. Make sure to expose yourselves to a variety of things that will provide mental nutrients that will better our lives in some form. We have to remember when no matter how old we get, when compared to the universe we are all children and children thrive off of what they are exposed to.

Processed: Before we jump into this discussion about processed media I want to explain that this will not be a one sided discussion where things are framed strictly to oppose this type of media. We have to look at things objectively in order to fully understand them without bias. Lets begin by describing what processed media is to better communicate this point. Of course all media has gone through one process or another before being viewed by the public. I'm speaking about this type of media in the same sense that I spoke on processed foods. These types of media are content that are saturated with unhealthy ingredients that slow up our processing of them. One would immediately reference reality tv as one of the main proponents of this style of media. Before we stigmatize all reality shows it's important to remind you of the positive forms of reality tv that were previously discussed as natural or clean media. With that on the table, lets dive into some of the processed foods that aren't quite as healthy for you, but may also serve a purpose.

Do you enjoy arguments and the draining residue they leave behind? If not, you are by far not alone. Most people despise this feeling and would much rather live their lives without this particular sensation. What becomes hard to understand is if his feeling is despised so much, why is it constantly watched by millions of people to the point of addiction. Watching arguments on television and the internet has captivated the minds of viewers world over. These processed forms of media can stagnate your life and become more draining than they are sources of energy, very similar to the unhealthy foods we consume. The main difference is we aren't able to physically see the negative results as easily. Think about this for a second, if the media that we consume helps to shape our minds and also our conversations, what exactly is it that we have to share? The saying that negative news travels faster than positive news is a very true one. This dynamic shows us that it is much easier for people to consume this type of media as well as food and choosing cleaner options can become a difficult task for some. Before delving too deep into what is negative and what is positive, knowing that we all have different perspectives, we should simple rate the things we watch as negative or positive. This doesn't mean that we shouldn't watch what we deem negative. Its about recognizing it so that we can better control our consumption of them. After all, even someone who enjoys healthy clean eating can enjoy a slice of birthday cake to celebrate the birthday of a loved one. The rating is there so that we don't begin to live our lives solely off of birthday cake.

Mental Metabolism

What can be gained from doing nothing? Well, you're most like likely thinking the answer is nothing, however, in their case the answer is weight. Weight is what we gain when we do absolutely nothing. It is also what pulls us down restricting freedoms that should be afforded to us all. After addressing the importance of diet it is an absolute must to look at the equal importance of exercise. Lets take a look at one of the body's most important organs to fully explore the significance of exercise in our lives. The heart is responsible for continuously pumping blood throughout our bodies sustain us through our activities as well as inactivity. It is widely agreed that exercise is perfect for the heart because it keeps it strong and healthy. In other words, the heart gains strength from doing what it is supposed to do. This is very similar to the way we function as a whole. We gain strength from doing what we are supposed to do. When we look at our metabolisms we can easily see that the people that engage in the most activity are in better shape from their counterparts who live a life of loafing. This isn't to be taken into extremes by only picturing a full fledge couch potato and comparing the to a triathlon runner to avoid seeing yourself in the scenario. This accounts for all activity, down to simply cleaning your surroundings. People that have very neat and cared for living conditions are often in better physical shape due to the strengthening of their metabolism from movement. The lethargic nature of lugging around extra weight should serve as an incentive to become more active and shed ourselves of what keeps us stagnant. It is this incentive that creates our mental metabolism.

What our mental metabolism consists of is the way our minds breakdown and process the information given to it. How long we allow the things we consume to linger in our mental reservoir depends on the functionality of our mental metabolism. When our bodies process the foods we consume they hold on to the nutrients the body requires and discards the rest as waste. When we intake too much fatty foods or foods that have little to no nutritional value our bodies will then store the fat and eliminate the waste left behind. This effects our physical state by slowing us down with with foods that don't provide the proper nutrition to transform into useful energy. This process occurs with our mental state as well. If the food for thought that we consume is lacking in nutritional value it will clog our systems and begin to store damaging materials in our minds. What we watch and listen to helps to formulate our mental diet. Taken in too much of these negative influences can make us mentally stagnant forcing progressive influences away from you in the process. It isn't too often that we find people that live a life of fitness and activity spending excessive amounts of time with people that live lives of obesity and lethargy. We all have unique taste and desires and have to adjust them at different times to achieve the desired results. However, it's important to remember that we are not alone in this world and the desires of others may not not always coincide with our own. We should remain mindful of the conversations and media that we ingest. Make a concerted effort to find the food for thought that creates the least amount of waste and adds fuel to the way we function. Watching negative content that leaves you discussing the negativity rather than productivity is extremely similar to eating foods that the body has trouble digesting. Controlling our diets is something that will remain beneficial to us throughout the course of our lives.

Mental Muscle Growth

Whether we admit it or not, we are all looking to grow in some way, shape, form, or fashion. Some of us want to grow spiritually, some in wealth of knowledge, others in wealth or monetary gain, the point is we are looking to see growth in some aspect of our lives. It is this growth that serves us as a marker in time by letting us know the status of our progress. When we look into the actual concept of growth we will find some key information of how we can apply some of its principles to our own lives. Lets take a look at the process of growing a small plant and see what useful information we can extract from the process. After all, we see the results of growth, but watching something actually grow is almost impossible for anyone to notice.

Step One: The Decision

Unless someone knocks on your door with all the materials required to grow a plant and you accept the gift and the challenge, you most likely won't be growing anything unless you've decided to do so on your own. Don't allow others to confuse inspiration and motivation with what you've decided to do. What I mean by this is often people around us will say things like "They're just doing that because they saw so and so did that" or something that effect in attempts to discount or devalue your efforts. The truth is it doesn't matter if they are absolutely correct, if you succeed in doing what you set out to do the motivation is of no consequence to others as long as you achieve your desired result.

Life Application

In life we will find that the decision is always the most important step of all. Because the decision stage is not visible to others it represents the inception period. This is the time before conception and more importantly this is when your new reality has been born. If you've made the decision to begin a healthy new lifestyle, even if you've decided that you will begin tomorrow, the truth is that you have already begun. The moment the idea comes into your head and you asses it and come to a decision to act on it you have already begun and everything that comes after whether good or bad is merely a part of the process. This information is pivotal in regards to your mental health when beginning any new endeavor. Knowing this gives us the confidence to strive for greatness amongst those that are already great. For example, if I wanted to become a painter and had no experience in painting, once I made the decision that I was going to go forward with this course of action, I have already become a painter before painting my first painting. The fact that I'm thinking about painting a picture tomorrow and decided to do so makes me a painter. We have to be careful not to confuse time doing something and the quality of work with defining ourselves in our current positions. This is where the phrase "you can be anything" comes from. It doesn't mean you should be talking about your future endeavor as if you're already Picasso, but it also doesn't mean you should devalue your dreams or the process that you've already begun. This is your life and once you've made a decision to become something or do something the only person that can stop you is you.

Step Two: The Materials

Unfortunately for certain lazy individuals like myself in part, we do not live in a world of magic. We have to physically port our dreams into existence. What this means is yes, we do have to purchase something. Possibly you may get lucky and be gifted with certain materials, but for the most part successful people are resourceful enough to get things done on their own. This isn't meant to insult those that have help acquiring what they need. I'm merely pointing out that the acquisition of the the things that we need to succeed is a trait of the successful. This doesn't mean to be a fool and look a gift horse in the mouth. I'm rather reminding you that your success will lie at the end of your own hands. Longevity cannot rely on others sourcing what you need to succeed. If it does you will have to ask yourself "are you truly successful". When you made the decision to leap out into a new venture, using others a safety net means that they will share in your success. This isn't always a bad thing, but you have to remain honest about that fact to fully own success.

Life Application

After the very important decision stages we've now entered the first stage of action. Understanding what physical things are necessary to bring our dreams into reality and acquiring them is beginning of the physical manifestation of our thoughts. I like to refer to this as the "put your money where your mouth is" stage. When others see you you with your potting soil, pots, watering cans etc the decision that you have made will now be on display for all to see and so will your success or failure. More important than displaying your efforts is for you to physically touch the materials that will build your dream. This brings your dream into full reality by allowing you to literally feel the sensation of touching and building your dreams. Eventually all of the materials you've purchased will become old, how they are used in the process is up to you. Referring back to our earlier painting reference, I bet people will begin to see your decision in the physical world once you acquired brushes, paints and a canvas, but more importantly you will begin to believe in yourself, which is crucial to your success.

Step Three: The Planting

Now we've arrive at the time for us to combine our vision with the materials we've provided. This is were the seed meets the solid in the pot we've made available. We have no control over certain aspects of the results, but so far we are on the right track to bringing fourth a new existence. Whether a local rabbit will interrupt our process or the weather takes an unsightly turn for the worst, we have met our first goal of merging the mental with the physical with the aspiration of conjoining the two. We are now on the road to success. Without the certainty of knowing if we will arrive at our destination, our chances are a hundred percent more likely than if we were not on the road at all. Remember to embrace the feelings, good or bad as you begin the creation of your physical vision and be proud of each step and milestone you reach, for these are your badges of honor and they should be mentally displayed proudly at all times.

Life Application

Fitting for this discussion, its now time to get down and dirty. There is no such thing as failure in these first three steps. That's the good thing, the bad is this is where many people begin to lean towards failure out of the fear of the unknown. Things in the physical world almost always feel different than in the state of our dreams. The laws of the world we live in do not exist in our dreams. We aren't held done by gravity and don't have to deal with other laws that dictate possibilities in the physical realm. However, in life these things do play a part in getting things done. Putting our hands in the dirt gives us a sense of the real life work that is required to manifest our dreams. Although this stage and the previous ones are void of failure, they are prone to discouragement. Sometimes the reality of the physical sensation is enough to deter us from continuing, bringing about the "what was I thinking" feeling that prevents so many of us from reaching our full potential. All of these thoughts are normal and that is why this stage is void of failure. You cannot fail in the first steps. Success and failure comes later. This is how we can determine whether you your first steps were a stumble or if you started off in the wrong direction altogether. While some of us may simply hit the ground running, others must learn to endure the new sensations as a part of the dream, and if failure occurs we have to learn to fail forward, meaning learn from your mistakes while continuing on, remembering that one day it will be something to laugh at. Even if your first painting doesn't come out the way you intended and your struggling to figure out why, remember you now have the struggles of a painter. Why? Because you are a painter, that's why!

Step Four: The Nurturing

Once we've planted our seeds in the soil and position them for sunlight, we begin the nurturing process. They won't water themselves. Unless you physically water them or position them to receive rainfall your plants won't receive the proper amounts of water to facilitate life. It is the maneuvering and care that you provide to this project that is classified as nurturing. For the first time in our process we are confronted by the chance of success or failure. The good thing is that the outcomes lies mostly within our control. Nurturing our decisions will better the scenarios that we create for ourselves. We also have to remain mindful of our approach to avoid providing the wrong amounts of what we consider nurturing. This is when we begin to get in our own way and in some cases end up being our own biggest obstacle. The chances of this happen are in most instances unlikely because the nature of caring in itself requires thought and thoughtfulness. These two functions help to create the right balance to nurture correctly.

Life Application

I've previously stated that the decision was the most important stage of all and I stand by that, it now I must introduce you the the most important of the reading four physical steps which is the nurturing. Many obstacles will surface once you begin to do something. I like to think of them as tests of if I'm deserving enough to receive what I desire. To some that may just be some philosophical bs to justify the real life bs that is interrupting my process. However, when you are doing something, there is no interruption of the process. Everything that happens is another part of the process. Having to reposition your plant due to not receiving enough sunlight is apart of the process. Checking for animals digging up your plant is also a part of the process. Realizing that you may not have purchased the right equipment specific to your needs might also be a part of the process. Learning and adjusting to these obstacles is the root of the nurturing process. How we adjust depends on how much we care and how much we care depends on how serious we are about seeing our dreams become a physical reality. When we care, the things and people around us are cared for and this is how we receive a positive result. This separates the things we simply want from the things we care about. The key is to care about the things we want because that will force us to nurture them into existence. Because of this fact, success and failure lies in the confines of this step. Unless catastrophic, circumstances should dictate your outcome. While in your nurturing stages circumstances should be addressed firmly and swiftly by you the creator of your dreams. Remember if your baby catches a cold, don't blame the weather, blame the nurturer for not getting a coat. I'm not at all saying that a baby that is cared for cannot get sick, I'm saying that the chances of your baby getting sick drastically decrease while being cared for.

Step Five: Enjoying the Fruit

This final step will not be explained with a separate life application because it is a life application. With full knowledge that failure was a definite possibility, it is more than fair that we enjoy the fruits of our labor whether bitter or sweet. Meaning if we see ourselves all the way thru a particular venture we should take pride in the journey no matter what the outcome. If you choose to continue you will only be bettering yourself while in the process of creating processes. The bottom line is that choosing to bring something into existence is a powerful process and equally as powerful responsibility. If you manage to bring your vision to life don't allow anyone to take away your moment in the sunshine, and that includes you. Sometimes we can get caught up in the critique of where we may have fallen short and forget to celebrate the experience. Its the small reflection that lead to the larger ones. We all have to start somewhere. Mark the milestones of your journey by tasting the fruits of your labor and design. As you begin to collect your milestones you'll see the value of them rivals some of the earth's most precious.

Summary

The point of this chapter is to help you to understand that your physical and mental health both require attention and maintenance. When we begin to exhibit care, the world of positive possibilities will begin to extend itself to us. This type of care is displayed by working to remain physically and mentally fit to protect the oasis we've created. The negativity kept out by the borders of our sanctuary comes in many forms and is only let in or out by you, the guard. Learning to guard and manage our mental metabolism helps us to discard waste and toxins from our lives mentally which will ultimately translate to the way our physical body responds. Keep your mind and body energized with positive nutrients that won't stagnate our growth and development. Where the mind goes the body will follow and both are ultimately under your control.

Chapter Five
Using the Elements

U nderstanding the elements can bring about an extraordinary turn of events in your life. Not only are these elements all around you, but they are what composes our very make up. Learning more about their uses and capabilities, helps you to further take advantage of your place in the world. Let's be honest, for those of us living in inner city environments, this concept might take a little bit more attention before fully understanding, but that fact in itself is one of the purposes of Feng Shui. It revolves around the placement of objects and elements. The clutter combined with the rapid pace attributable to most modern cities makes understanding what is not directly affecting your daily activities in the conscious mind sometimes hard to relate to. It involves slowing down a pace to be able to internalize concepts that are often ignored and deemed cooky or weird. When we begin to understand how things apply to our lives, it gives us an incentive to learn more about them. Things we don't deem necessary are often discarded to the waste-side and replaced by what is necessary or mere indulgences. Let's take this excellent opportunity the universe has presented us with to explore some new concepts that can help us to better understand the world we exist in.

We know that the periodic table of elements consists of ninety-nine elements in total, luckily for us the ancient art of Feng Shui is constructed with five, making it far easier for us to explore in this book. So, what are the five elements that I've been speaking of? We have Wood, Fire, Earth, Metal, and Water and as I've previously stated, the elements exist not only around us but inside of us as well. The existence of these elements outside of us is in no way debatable, yet the thought of them being inside of us may raise a few eyebrows when addressing this particular phenomenon. Pay close attention to this section as it may prove to be one of the most powerful things you've read in association with the lifestyle of a city slicker. It is not only about the elements themselves, but it speaks to the functionality and process of these elements when working in conjunction with one another. Let's briefly explore a process that we are all familiar with to give context to what will be presented in this chapter.

In this example, we will take a look at part of the life cycle of a plant. First we will begin by organizing our ingredients, soil, water, sunlight, the seed, and nature itself. Our sample plant cannot grow with these ingredients. It creates a formula of functionality. The soil is necessary for the nutrients it will give our seed, the water for the nutrients and moisture it provides and the sunlight is used to split the water molecules to extract the oxygen and give to the plant. This process is known as photosynthesis, but for the sake of simplifying things here we will simply refer to it as nature. All other the things in this example have an individual power in themselves, but when working in combination with each other create something equally and in some instances more powerful than the individual elements. How does this relate to this topic? When it comes to the elements of Feng Shui that exist immediately around us, learning to put them into their proper position will create cycles rendering us as the element of nature in our previous example. We will be the force or the process that activates these elements to work in conjunction with one another. Lets now clear out our minds of the clutter of preconceived notions and prejudices and leave room for the concepts to flow in and work in connection with you the reader to activate new perspectives on how we live and exist in our own environments.

Wood

What can be learned from observing wood as an elemental factor of Fen Shui. Well, we must first take a look at the substance itself and its unique attributes before attempting to understand why it was chosen as an element to begin with. What is wood and why is what it represents valuable enough to find itself on the short list of valuable elements? I'll begin by section if off this substance into different categories to make this topic easier to explore. By the way, the way this topic is broken into different parts and structured to allow its true meaning to flow into your mind without confusion is a form of Feng Shui. You will understand this concept more and more as you continue to read and open your mind.

When we look at wood as a substance, what we will easily discover is that it has very bold traits that make it very easy to describe. The powerful substance known as wood is most notable for its quality of strength, but in its strength it also shows great flexibility. There are many ways in which wood and its properties can be used to enhance our lives in the physical state. However here we are looking to apply its traits and principles to enhance the functionality of our minds. Lets again open our minds to the possibilities of something new and hopefully discover a jewel to covet while embarking on a new journey. Yes, the pun was intended!

Strength

The building capabilities of wood have been known to man probably since the existence of early man. Wooden hand tools have been discovered from just about every early civilization to grace the planet. That's correct wooden tools have been used to make other things from actual wood as well. Hear we have a substance powerful enough to be used on itself and bring things into creation. If left alone in the woods one would quickly discover the powerful nature of wood in all of its forms. While alone in the woods you would also quickly discover the need for shelter and would most likely want to build it out of the most powerful substance available to you, which would more than likely be wood. Here you will find yourself submitting to the power of wood while entrusting it to safeguard you while you rest and protect you from the elements as well as intrusion. When we break things down to the simplest form possible it makes it easier for us to find the value in it, not because I said so, that's math doing the talking. When we approach physical elements from a mental perspective we have to look at what it does for us physically and mentally apply the properties to our lives. When we build with would we recognize its strength and mentally recognizing our own strength will also serve us well in the constructing of ourselves.

Fung Shway

Flexibility

One of the more powerful things we can learn from studying wood is its flexible nature. Imagine something as strong as would still having the ability to soften and bend. Strong enough to support you, yet flexible enough to bend to your will, sounds like what we look for in the people we interact with. This is a clear sign that we are on the right track. It's no coincidence that the properties of this substance sound like the human interactions that we encounter on a daily basis. The power of strength does not come with flexibility. Flexibility is a unique trait that is not attached to strength, but when coupled with it brings more power and significance to that strength and flexibility in the process. Imagine a powerful person that has no ability to flex. This person will be described by their strength in ways that garner respect for only that specific reason. Their lack of flexibility can lock them into a submission hold, trapping them with the very strength they consist of. It's similar to the way that we view football players or wrestlers, we can easily bare witness to their size and power but it is the flexibility of their movement that makes them good at what they do. Without flexibility you can find yourself outmaneuvered by someone less powerful yet more agile than you using your power against you. However, it should be noted that too much flexibility can lead to a break. All substances have a breaking point and if pushed in a particular direction will break. It is up to us to remain flexible but study the limits of our own flexibility as well as the limits of those around us to ensure that we are not approaching our breaking points or pushing someone else to theirs.

Intuition

Something as powerful and as flexible as wood leads to intuition. It's similar to clay in that regard because of the instinctive nature it evokes. It is a substance that is full of potential by nature. Although wood has the capabilities of being sturdy and fortified, its principles are rooted in creativity. We have to remember to use our sturdiness to further our creative goals rather than becoming a victim of our own strength. Focusing on the creation of new ideas and bringing them into existence comes from the same intuitive nature of working with wood. Understanding these principles will only further you in your endeavors.

Condensed - Creativity

When applying the principles of Feng Shui to our lives wood represents our creatives forces. Taking on the nature of wood means to exhibit strength and flexibility for the purpose of building. It would be completely disingenuous for me to not mention the other nature of would and how this can effect adversely to the way we set out for. You also find would to be at times as rigid as it is smooth. Things that are rigid in nature are often hard to work with and can add unwanted complexities to otherwise simple tasks. When we find ourselves working in this capacity we are also using the nature of wood, however, it is now working against us oppose to for us. Wood also can flourish in the form of a great Red Wood tree representing possibility at its highest level, or it can also be stubborn in nature like a stump in the ground that is also made of the very same wood. Being stubborn should not always be considered a bad thing because it is necessary at times, but a stump in the ground represents inflexibility which is oppose to creation because it will be what it will be. The lack of flexibility creates a lack of creativity. This doesn't render the stump in the ground useless, it rather limits its capabilities, which limits its possibilities thus stunting its creative growth. Keep in mind all of the aspects of wood when using your creative mind and things will begin to flourish for you as well.

Fire

Let's take a look at what happens when oxygen meets carbon and creates an extremely useful substance called fire. This particular substance when applied to Feng Shui represents the fire burns inside of us fueling the creativity harnessed inside of us. Some believe that there is an actual fire burning inside of us turning the oxygen we breathe in into the carbon we breathe out, but the fire we'll be focusing on creates the burning of desire. The fire that is lit beneath you to inspire activity is also the fire that is lit inside of you. Just as someone in the woods may light a fire to keep warm and find different ways to keep the fire lit, we will also have to find ways of keeping our fire lit in our own lives. In finding mental ways to keep our fire burning we will also discover what truly motivates us and how to fuel that motivation to stay inspired. Even the things that we do well and easily can transform into a boring and draining task if we don't have the proper motivation to carry them out correctly.

It is now time to do as Jay Z says jump "fresh out the frying pan into the fire" to find out whether we would like to fuel our fire or put it out. Fire is an extremely powerful element in the fact that when it burns uncontrollably it can burn everything making ashes of everything that surrounds it. This can also occur with the fire hat we are speaking about if not controlled and contained. The fire inside of us must be harnessed and used at will for it to become an energy source. Looking at the largest ball of burning gas that we know of, the sun, we can see that the very same fire that sustains life on our planet will literally incinerate anything that gets close enough to it rendering fire the gift and the curse. Lets take some time to examine the gift while not ignoring the curse to see if we can better ourselves in the process.

Inspiration

What can be said about inspiration? Well first we should all understand that it is a unique process. Everyone has different motivations for the things they do in life. It may range anywhere from talent to revenge, yet if used in the right way will lead to the same result. Imagine for a second that you are attempting sit down on a chair an inadvertently end up sitting on a flame of fire. Unless you have absolutely no feeling in lower body, you will most likely leap out of your seat as a reaction to the burning sensation your experiencing on your second set of cheeks. This should add a visual to the fire provoking action. That fire will not allow you to sit down comfortably. It forces you into being motivated enough to do something. How can we apply this to our everyday lives for our benefit? Well for starters we should identify what we are looking for the way we discussed previously in Chapter Three. Our dreams and desires are exactly what keeps this fire lit and contained. When a goal of ours is accomplished or even altered the degree of the fire will also be altered according to how we feel.

They are different types of inspiration. Some may assume that being inspired by negativity will render you negative but this is simply not the case. Science proves that energy can not be destroyed, only changed. This means that negative energy can be turned positive and the reverse is also true for positive energy. Revenge in itself might not be a positive force yet if used correctly can be transformed into a positive energy source. There is a distinction between revenge and outright malicious negative behavior. Revenge doesn't have to mean physical harm or seeing someone in a negative position. I'm speaking on revenge that leans more toward the aspect of vindication. When we find ourselves in a position where someone has a negative view of us, we can choose to fall victim to this by becoming discouraged and allowing our fire to be extinguished, rather than using that negative energy to fuel the desire for the success we are looking for. It is often said that success is the best revenge making revenge the fuel for the newly acquired success.

The bottom line is that we should all be looking for some form of success in our lives, no matter how minuscule. These successes are determined by our desire to achieve them and that alone. As long as desire burns inside of us we are being motivated to achieve success. Positive energy will always push you towards where you're looking to go, but that doesn't mean that negative energy can't be used to do the same. In one case you have a lit fire burning inside of a house forcing its occupants to run outside, while another home also has a lit fire burning. However, the fire in the second home is burning inside of a fireplace in a controlled setting allowing the fire burn as fire does while the energy harnessed from it proves to be more useful than not.

Expressiveness

The ability to express yourself can sometimes emulate an explosion. The nature of expressiveness is a big and powerful force. When most people think of expressing themselves without limitations they often think of expressing themselves in the biggest way possible. This energy can be stifled by the shy nature of some of us that prevents us from lighting up the room in the way we feel to. Removing what's blocking us from accomplishing these things is not always possible. The fire that we've lit previously is the very same fire that lights the fuse to the bomb of our expression. Expression is sometimes suppressed by the feelings of others that surround a particular situation. When we think of expressing ourselves we have to view it like a bomb that we are planning to ignite and survey the premises first. However, if you're intending to express yourself in a positive way, you can comfortably light the fuse and express yourself. Whether its an idea that you're expressing or something you've already accomplished you should try to express yourself with as little limitations as possible. That's one of the benefits of being positive and thinking positive. When its time to express yourself you don't have to hold yourself back being worried about negative reactions to what you're presenting. If someone turns what you've expressed into a negative for them you have to remember that's their option and they've made their choice. Try to remember when you're in a positive state of being the desire to share that positivity in the form of expression is that very same fire we've been speaking of. Be positive and express yourself and if you aren't thanked for it remember to thank yourself.

Boldness

One thing that can be said of fire is that is definitely a bold force. It is something that cannot be denied, only fueled, extinguished, or avoided. The presence of fire is noticeable by anyone that comes anywhere near it. It forces any living thing into a state of awareness and acknowledgement of its presence. When it comes to emulating the nature of fire its boldness is certainly one of the attributes to admire. Boldness can be tamed, yet when unleashed is as powerful as it chooses to be. With that in mind we should all be aware that the fire or boldness that lies inside of us is being controlled, tamed, an unleashed at our own discretion. We have the ability to be as bold as we desire, because that boldness comes from our desire. Even a shy person will shout out and try to get the attention of everyone around if in the presence of danger. This lets us know that the ability to express ourselves always lies within and can be unleashed at any moment, boldly and proudly to whoever wherever we are.

Condensed - Ambition

If we condensed the nature of fire and apply it to our mental state of Feng Shui it can be summed up by one word, ambition. Ambition is a burning flame that keeps us moving in the face of adversity by fueling our progression. Because any flame can be extinguished we have to protect and guard this flame from going out.

Also, we have to remain aware that fire can turn on us and when it does we too can be burned. When our own fire burns inside of us and is uncontrolled it shows itself in the form of rage, and aggression, and in that rage we can easily lose focus. It creates the type of impulsiveness that is scattered without direction and leaves everything remaining in scorched ashes from the flames that went rogue. Ambition is something we all have, its the degree of ambition that differs from person to person. People who display their ambition are generally positive in the fact that they express their own desires giving them a greater chance at achieving them. Ambition is just as powerful as the fire that represents it and should be treated accordingly. We understand that the very fire we tell children to stay away from out of fear of them being burned is also lit and used in the very same home we tell them this in. Remember to use the fire and not be used by it. Protect your flame and fuel it when needed and it will serve you as a tool rather than one more adversary to face.

Earth

Yes, we are speaking about the third rock from the sun, but not in its entirety. We are actually focusing on one fourth of the planet that we call earth and ironically that one fourth we are speaking about is affectionately known as earth. That's right, we're focusing on the ground and what it represents to us and how it manifests in our lives. When we look at the earth, the soil, the rock, the actual ground we can find magnificent structure that in no way, shape, or form appeared over night. The principles we can extract from the earth give us the footing we need to navigate through this physical realm.

Fung Shway

Without that footing we are literally floating in space making it a little more difficult to accomplish things physically. The earth itself is a part of our solar system rendering the earth in space. Thinking that we're on earth and not in space is a backwards notion and a detrimental distortion of reality. The fact is that we are in space, the earth included as we've discussed earlier in this book and the mental application of the earth's principles will include its cosmic nature as well.

Lets take the time in the time to explore as well as appreciate our earth and all that it provides for us while on this journey of self exploration. Whether you believe the earth is flat or round is of no consequence. One thing that most rational minds can agree on is that we are on the earth and that it should be respected and revered because our physical existence is greatly influenced by the health of the earth. Now that the premise has been laid down lets stand firmly on it as we do our own earth and begin this exploration to see what can be extracted from the foundation and used to better our lives.

Grounding

What does it mean when we say we are "down to earth"? Shouldn't that be apparent if we are standing on the surface of the earth? Well, this may be humanity's way of subconsciously understanding our existence. The phrase "down to earth" acknowledges our cosmic side by figuratively inferring that we are not floating around aimlessly, but rather firmly rooted in reality. This isn't saying that floating through space represents a bad or negative thing, because all of the elemental principles are applicable at different times and in different instances. What it is saying is that they are rooted in times when being rooted is required. The ground represents foundation. This foundation is the platform we use to build our ideas and bring our visions into existence. Being grounded is what adds order to our thoughts because it order to build soundly we need to first have a surface to do so. Our thoughts and ideas serve as the blueprint for our building while being grounded provides a place to accomplish what we initially set out to achieve.

No matter how deep in love we fall with the dream state that we enter in our sleep, we have to acknowledge the laws of this existence, and gravity is one of the most important ones to focus on. Gravity shows us that no matter how long we find ourselves suspended in the air we will eventually have to come back down to the surface and become grounded for some period of time. Being grounded doesn't mean that we have to remain grounded. It is where we root ourselves to remember where we are and what we are looking to accomplish. All of the ideas we are looking to bring fourth into existence consists of the materials that lie beneath our feet in the earth. This is the main purposes of being grounded. When you are mentally grounded you have to remember to respect your position as well as what it provides. Your building blocks consists of the very ground we stand on.

Balance

Why is it that we are so amazed when we see someone walking on a tightrope? Well, the obvious answer is because its far easier to balance ourselves while walking on the flat earth. This is precisely why one of the principles we've extracted from examining the earth is balance. The seesaw exemplifies the nature of balance and will be discussed later in this book in greater detail. However, for now we can focus on the middle of the seesaw that is resting on the surface of the earth. This part of the seesaws structure is perhaps the most important part and is only useful with the existence of a surface. Lets take a look at the aspect of balance that refers to our equilibrium as opposed to the Yin and Yang universal aspect we will discuss later.

In our younger years we've all experienced a fall at one point or another. Before and during that fall we feel a rush of being completely out of control and having little options available to us in that moment. Most of us do our best to brace ourselves for the impact of the fall in hopes that it wont injure us as a result. That out of control rush is what we try to avoid with the presence of balance. When situations in our lives begin to spiral "out of control" we need to implement the principles of the earth and ground ourselves to regain balance in what we are doing. These are the points when we need to slow down, sometimes even stop to asses the ground we stand on and make sure our foundation is secure for what we need it for. However, it is key to keep in mind that balance is a tool like any other, while it is useful it is not always applicable. Some situations require us to let go and fly the course, but remembering the ground is always there to support us if need be.

Stability positioning

The purpose of building anything is lost if what is built is not stable. The earth represents other things but stability happens to be one of its most important aspects for us as living physical beings. The fastest way to get where you want to go is to understand and respect where you are. Even for those that want to take flight must understand and respect the stability of the ground. This is why a runway is designed as a smooth and flat surface, because that stability is what enables you to take flight. Pilots are used for 'flying" planes, yet I'm sure if placed on jagged unstable runway they would take issue with that. They understand that the runway is how they gather enough speed to lift off of the ground and also ensures a smooth landing when its time to return. Stability is also to be embraced when needed and not relied on as an absolute. When we view things as absolutes we negate other elements that may serve us more practically at the time we need them. As humans, stability is something that helps us to also feel secure and its in our nature to seek out that security. With this being the case, that secure feeling can hinder us from exploring new options and ways of doing things and leave us in a state of stagnation. Remember if stability was supposed to remain constant, man would have never taken flight. We would have no reason to leave the ground.

Condensed Safety

When we condense the principles of the earth into one it becomes apparent that the overall principle of the earth is safety. The stability it provides to enable us to be firmly grounded while staying in balance gives us the safety we all desire as humans. There is a risk and reward factor we need to review before leaving this principle. With risk comes reward and in many instances the greater the risk the greater the reward. Safety and stability lower our level of risk and in that absence of risk we can become open to some of the negative sides of this element. Boredom, sluggishness, and being too serious are now on the table when we place ourselves in risk free environments for extended periods of time. When the risk is greater than the reward boredom will ultimately prove itself as a better option. However, these choices have to be weighed and timed to make them of any use to us. Boredom and stability entails a lack of action and its the action that actually gets things done. Understanding this fact will make boredom more of a useful tool rather than something that festers and provokes the wrong type of action. There lies a huge difference between doing nothing and being still and being still is a tactic. The earth signifies the thought before the action. It's a place where can pit stop while remaining stable and balanced before deciding how to proceed. Picture to people sitting at opposite ends of a chessboard with neither one of them moving. From the outside looking in I think its safe to assume that no one would describe them as doing nothing. There lack of activity is the proper use of the earth element. Life and the game of chess have been compared since the inception of the game and rightfully so. Remember this in regards to the earth and the safety it provides because when you're standing on solid ground there's no need for a net.

Metal

Lets take a look at the most weaponized of all the elements, metal. Yes, there are many different types with many different uses ranging from a sword of steel to using gold as a conductor. One thing is for sure, the presence of metal will force us into being more alert and aware of our surroundings. It promotes concentration and development of skill simply by being in the presence of it. While metals exist inside of our earth the things that are produced from these metals come from man. People tend to treat metal as if it was an unnatural substance and that couldn't be further from the truth. We sometimes look at metal with disdain because it is sometimes synonymous with being man made. My suggestion is that you tell tat to your doctor the next time they tell you that you need more iron. When you discover that you can add more iron to your body by eating more green leafy vegetables you will begin to further understand the connection between all of these elements and how they work together.

Lets carefully take a look at the nature and principles that exist inside of the precious metals of the earth. The word we will be focusing on is carefully, because that is what is attached to working with metals of any kind. Understanding metal and its properties is also understanding the properties and nature of ourselves. Using our senses, lets take a keen eye to this principle, again extracting hidden jewels awaiting our discovery. It's now time to get off of these pins and needles and dive in to this element and yes, that pun was also intended.

Logic

When describing these elements there is nowhere more applicable to apply logic than to the principles of metal. Most of the tools we use in the physical world come from the earth's metals. These metals can be sharpened and used to cut, or simply used for their weight to apply blunt force. Which ever way we choose to use these metals because of the danger that can occur when working with them logic becomes pivotal. The reason we wouldn't leave small children in the presence of these metals is due to their lack of discernment required to function in that type of environment. One thing we can all agree on is working with metal takes skill and practice and in order to acquire the skill set needed your sense of logic must be heightened. If we are in the presence of someone waving around a feather in the air our presence of mind would be a lot different than if we were in the presence of someone waving around a sword. This shouldn't be at all hard to comprehend how logic sets in when in the company of these metallic instruments. When in some forms of danger it's human nature to panic. However, in the presence of danger the enemy of logic is to panic. The random irrational movements of panicking add to the danger you are facing. We must remain as logical as the principle of metal dictates.

Remember this is about applying the physical attributes of this element to our mental state. This is not referring to simply working around or with metals, its about making these principles relevant in our everyday lives and knowing when is the best time to implement them and that is logic. The answer to many of the problems that exists in our lives is rooted in the presence of logic. Logic is our ability to tie these elements together. Placing our minds in a logical state should come after the illogical state of dreaming. Our dreams and visions aren't meant to be logical. Logic comes into play when trying to pull these visions into reality. In order to build in a physical world and protect what we've built we might find ourselves building with metal and also locking the door with a metal lock when the structure is complete.

Focus

Focus is also an important feature attributed to the element of metal. Because metal has a serious nature associated with it focus is key when working with any metal to ensure our safety and the safety of others. In the same way that our ability to implement logic is heightened, the same occurs in regards to our level of focus. The metallic element represents the presence of focus in the things we need to do out of necessity. Focus is required in most of the things that we do, but not all. There are some things that we do where we are guided by our own intuition and applying focus will actually effect us negatively. However, there are many instances where we need to either be full focused or make allowance for time to refocus and asses our situation and what it is we are trying to accomplish. The focus that comes from the metal element is what you are seeing when watch some juggle swords. It is also what you see when you watch someone being responsible in there own lives and bringing their tasks and projects to completion.

Whether we choose to admit it or not, focus is something that is often needed, but that doesn't stop it from being a skill that requires practice. Part of growing in this world is learning what is necessary and what isn't and practicing and honing the skills of the things that will be of the most use to us. Understanding the importance of focus is actually the easy part. The hard part is remaining focused and making sure not to focus on the wrong things. This is where the skill of focus is required because sometimes we find ourselves involuntarily focusing on negative things or people that can't help us in our situations. This shows us that application of focus is not the hard part, its the ability to apply it when and where its needed that requires skill. For some, focus is a talent and for others it is a skill. The good thing about this is that it is not an impossible feat to accomplish, you'll get better with practice.

Organization

Organization is often considered the arch enemy of the creative mind. The free thinking nature of creative people can sometimes prevent them from getting things out of the idea stage. If and when they do bring their ideas into fruition the time spent doing so could've been greatly decreased with the proper organizational skills. Metal reflects the organization principle because working with or producing these materials requires organization and classification. Walking into a disorganized factory can be disheartening, but a disorganized shop that works with metals can be more dangerous than disheartening. Organization is key to many aspects of our lives, but the most important of all doesn't lie in the physical world. The organization of our thoughts is how we get things done in a timely manner and in a way that will be most productive for us. Organization doesn't dictate your thoughts, it dictates your thought process. Every process requires organization on some level. Separating your thoughts into categories like emotional, practical, or ideal is an organization process. When we approach things logically we understand that we have to respect the process of things. This is what dictates the outcome.

Don't confuse having good intentions with having a process. Your intentions are tied to the outcomes you will receive. However, it is the process you employ that will allow you to see these results in real time in the real world. Organization also greatly helps you when it comes to having patience, because what makes patience easier to have is understanding the process. Anyone that has ever tracked a package can attest to the difference between just waiting and knowing that your package was scanned at a facility and is on the back of a truck and in route to you. Both scenarios require patience, but being aware of the process allows you to free up your thoughts and wait peaceful while things come your way.

Condensed Clarity

The condensed principle of metal is clarity. The different aspects of this principle we've reviewed when applied correctly will bring us to a state of clarity. Clarity doesn't infer that we will always have a positive result. Sometimes we have to understand that things don't always go according to plan, but in the presence of clarity we are able to understand why. The reason cleaning up is so important in our lives is because it gives us the clarity that we need to function at our highest level. It's no coincidence that a major part of cleaning a room is the organization process. Embracing the element of metal helps us to understand that before a tool can be of any use to us the must itself go through a process of completion. Metal is often treated as something separate from nature and this couldn't be further from the truth. First off, we must understand that nature itself is a process. Nothing in nature occurs instantly, especially the metals that form inside of the earth. These metals have gone through a multimillion year process before taking the form that we presently see them in. This is what renders metals as apart of nature, no different from any other.

The downside to the organized mind is over organizing. This can make us overly critical of others who may not possess the ability put things in order in the same ways that we do. Also, we don't want to become too analytical studying processes and forgetting to live while doing so. It is possible to overshoot your goal by analyzing things to much and shooting past the point of clarity only to end up in another state of confusion. When creating or studying certain processes take your time in the same way that you would if you were working around sharp metals. Remember that processes exist all around us, even creating a process is a process, but don't think about that one too long.

Water

The late great Bruce Lee famously stated "be like water". This was an extremely powerful application when dealing with the mental application of Feng Shui, because it simplified the very complex nature of martial arts by using one of the earth's most powerful elements to exemplify how to move. Looking back at of the elements that we've discussed it should be noted that water has the ability to soften or weaken wood, extinguish fire, erode the earth, and rust metal. In the minds of some people this would render water the most powerful of al of the elements. However, Feng Shui is about respecting all of these elements equally, similar to the way all living things deserve respect regardless of their particular level of strength. Besides the fact that three fourths of this planet as well as three fourths of our bodies consists of water, water has many unique traits and principles that are worth examining. Whether its the ability to take any shape, or the ability to be concentrated and thrusted, water can exert softness or great power and this is what we will be focusing on to help us further understand the use of this element.

Water is an extremely influential part of our makeup in the physical world. Life itself cannot exist without the presence of water. Before birth we are all creatures of water, but this isn't the only reason we have such a strong relationship with it. Existing in water is one thing, being like water is a total different one. Lets take a look at these magnificent principles of water to find how it can aid us the restructuring of our minds. With that being stated, lets waste no time and dive right into the subject at hand, and yes, that pun was also intended.

Wisdom

When we understand the concept of wisdom we understand that it can only occur after we are knowledgeable about something. Wisdom sets in when you have enough information or experience to visualize an outcome of an event that hasn't yet taken place. It has the ability to take the shape necessary at the given moment and more importantly understands why. Wisdom is not something that can be achieved overnight nor can it be forced. It happens on its own time and in the way that it decides on its own accord. Wisdom is best applied when applied to your own life. The first steps to applying wisdom in your own life is learning yourself in order to know yourself. Only then will wisdom be applicable, yet it wont require thought. That's the beauty of the nature of wisdom, it only requires what's innate. Once we acquire the right amount of knowledge and information wisdom will set in without any action required in the same way that water does not have to be instructed on what to do. The instruction stage is the stage of acquiring information. The more thought we put into things the more information we absorb. Wisdom is however is not the acquiring of information but the ability to apply it and the ability to know when to apply it.

The benefits that wisdom provides is one that keeps on giving. Your wisdom when transferred equals knowledge to someone else. We can't expect for the wisdom that we reflect to become wisdom for others. When someone receives information from us it takes them time to asses and actually live out that information. Only after living the information will wisdom set in. Wisdom is a living experience and information is alive. Despite what many people believe facts can and do change over the course of time. In an ever changing world its only natural for facts to change with it. Knowing and understanding this is also an application of wisdom. As adults there will always remain a part of us that remains in connection with are child mindset. It is only the experiences that we've had that separates us from children. The experiences we've received have given us the information needed to asses life in a different way than children. As we age we begin to understand that knowing is not always enough. This is the reason if you ask any adult if they would like to re-enter their teenage years knowing what they now know they would more than leap at the opportunity. These same individuals can share their information with a teenager and although it may help, the lack of life experience will make it impossible to understand to the point of having wisdom. Knowledge can help you to understand a concept, while wisdom will help you understand why.

Spirituality

The spiritual essence of water is perhaps its most intricate asset. Spirituality is not something that is easy to discuss without the obvious bs factor. Because we are addressing the unseeable, speaking on it should be done in the most practical way possible to avoid losing your attention with useless filler that won't serve anyone. When I speak of spirituality, I'm speaking about the connection to from the mind to our physical bodies. What this means is the understanding of the existence of a part of ourselves that is separate from our physical existence, yet still has an impact on it. This connection must be acknowledged in order to fully understand our composition. If we choose to think of ourselves as only physical we are denying our true nature and ignoring the major part of our being. This is in essence turning your back on yourself. Its leaving your physical body unguided by what is uniquely equipped to guide you. This is the voice that you've been hearing in your head since before birth, the real you. Having a connection with this voice inside of you is paramount on our journey on this planet. It creates more than an understanding, rather an "inner-standing" of ones self that can bring us to a state of completion. This connection is better described by the phrase "as above so below".

Water connects with this principle because of it's ability to move according to how a situation dictates while still maintaining its fluidity. Being able to flow into the right direction by having a connection with the force that guides you. More important than the actual current is the force behind the current. What is actually making the water flow? The unseen force behind our actions is known as insight and this insight is also one of the powerful attributes of water. When we reflect on the true aspects of water this is a key principle to keep in mind.

Condensed Flow

Condensing the principles of water into one principle will lead into the presence of a flow. When things flow for you it is a beautiful experience. It represents movement without thought, and this is what Bruce Lee was so masterful at accomplishing. This phenomenon isn't limited to to the art of combat. It exists in every aspect of our lives from the time we are born. On a smaller scale that flow begins at birth. Lets take for example the relationship between a mother and child. When the mother gives birth and the child reaches for the breast, it is doing so without instruction. No one has to tell the baby where to look for food. It is an innate action that requires no thought to receive the desired outcome. Things flow in our lives at different ties but flows are not constant. This is the nature of our physical existence. Time creates change and that change alters our universe both negatively and positively for us. Understanding that things change gives a greater chance of dealing with that change in the way that is best for us. Sometimes things flow for us in our love lives, or in business, or simply within our spirit giving us the an overall good feeling about our current state, but a major part of flow is understanding that at different stages of the river the current can and will change.

Anyone that has visited the ocean understands the power of a wave. Waves are a part of a lager flow and can give us the feeling of fighting to stay on our feet when confronted by them. This can happen to us with the flows that exist in our own lives. Sometimes when in the midst of a flow, without the use of a pit stop we can become overwhelmed by our own experiences. When overwhelmed we can become unbalanced and lose our footing giving us the feeling of going under water and struggling to catch our breath. When dealing with life in the general sense every flow isn't necessarily a positive one. Sometimes things are flowing for us in a negative way and this is the existence of a rut. It's at this point we have to stop what we are doing and remove ourselves from the waters in order to recalibrate our being to a state of positivity to eventually end up in a flow of positive energy.

Summary
Using the Elements

Wood: This element can be burned by fire, softened by water, works well with earth and can be penetrated by metal.

Fire: This element can be burned or fueled by wood, can be extinguished by water, can be smothered by the earth and has the ability to melt metals.

Earth: This element works well with wood, smothers fire, bonds with water, and can be penetrated or facilitate metals.

Fung Shway

Metal: This element can be rusted by water, penetrate or be smothered by the earth, melted by fire, or pierce wood.

Water: This element can be absorbed by the earth, contained by metal, extinguish fire, and softened wood.

The contents of this chapter should be meditated and reflected on in order to fully apply its use. When we understand the nature of these elements and what they represent in our lives we will gain access to more control over our lives by knowing which element to implement at a specific times to fuel or diffuse situations in our lives. Remember, when you comprehend the full scope of these elements it will be apparent that fighting fire with fire may not be the best option. When confronted by the raging flames of fire try looking to water for some relief rather than conjuring up more of what you are currently opposing.

Chapter Six
Self Building
& Wealth Building

I t is "abundantly" clear that now is the time to address the ever so prevalent correlation between self and wealth. That's right, we can set aside all of the cliches and rhetoric about money not being able to buy happiness, or we can address those issues head on exposing them for the cliches that are, once again removing the cluttering obstacles of falsities from our minds. Lets be honest, how does anyone plan to really do for self without addressing the issue of the price tag? That money can't buy happiness tag-line is only asserted by two sets of people, the rich and the poor. I've never witnessed someone winning the lottery and dawning a frown on the news. It is obvious that jumping up and down with the widest smile imaginable can easily be associated with winning the lottery. This is not by coincidence. Ignoring this reality is actually just that, ignoring reality. We have to be able to see clearly in anything we are attempting to become successful in and false realities have no place when attempting to do so.

Firstly, lets begin by destroying the myth. Money doesn't buy happiness. If money doesn't buy happiness, it will certainly buy a number of things that make us happy. It is what drives us in a modern society. Looking at the definition of happiness, it includes the words good fortune and prosperity in its description. This is not to say that the only way to achieve happiness is through monetary gain. It is more about being realistic about the outcomes in life we desire. Happiness is an emotion that we all experience at different times for different reasons. Knowing this makes it easier to grasp the concept of how to trigger this emotion in the right way to achieve the desired level of happiness. For instance, some of us may find ourselves in an utter state of elation through the act of giving. This is a noble stance, yet without anything to give they would find themselves looking for other ways to find happiness. Some of you might be saying "What's wrong with that?" The problem comes in with the fact that are now seeking a secondary route and giving up on finding true happiness.

The reason happiness is so closely associated with abundance is because within the abundance we will find options. The phrase "happy as a kid in a candy store" signals the delight provided by abundance. That particular reference I'm sure is not referring to a child in a store with one piece of candy. This may very well seem trivial to you, but it is extremely important to dispel cliches from our lives when they simply don't apply. They often serve as unwritten rules that create obstacles in our path to success and in this case success meaning happiness. Looking at money objectively, we can see that the need for it goes beyond our emotional perception of its use. What that means is, unless you are planning to completely withdraw from society, money will certainly be a factor in your existence on earth. What this doesn't mean is that we have to become solely driven by the concept of money allowing it to consume us totally. Being consumed with any type of concept can create a personal hell by leaving you to spend your existence chasing a carrot on a stick. Once again we find ourselves confronted with the secret of a healthy lifestyle, balance. Let's take an objective look at how to build wealth and self in a healthy fashion.

Step One - Acknowledgement

The power of acknowledgement is certainly the reason for it taking its place as the first step. Even in a race as long as a marathon, it all begins with the first step. Referring back to what we've learned about the construction of our dreams will help us to see the necessity for honesty in our lives. An honest approach to looking at money will open your mind to create the room required to actually receive. After the acknowledgment, you are then able to begin the process of moving past where you are to where you want to be. When you assess what you want from life you can properly strategize how to accomplish your goals without compromising your integrity. By bearing witness to our own desires we can transfer the energy attached to working for someone, to the energy associated with working for ourselves. When we organize our goals, you will never work for anyone other than yourself again. This doesn't mean you won't have to physically go to work or have a supervisor or boss. It means whether entrepreneurship or a conventional occupation your mind will understand that you're physical body is really working for your mind to achieve the desired level of comfort for your physical existence and that is very different than simply working for a boss.

Step Two - Planning & Commitment

After acknowledging your desires comprehensively you find yourself at the moment of action. Your desires will dictate your actions to moving towards them effectively. This step of planning and commitment is completely in sync with the operation of your oasis. Your financial stability and your mental stability can in many ways become one in the same. Although your financial stability can lean heavily on your mental health, your social skills and self esteem can also play heavily into your overall mental health. However, we must acknowledge the role financial freedom plays in giving us the options to feel the freedom it provides. Planning financially and making a commitment to follow through is simply the act of following through on the realistic side of your desires to achieve them in real time. Planning to succeed and committing to it is far different than using phrases like "it is what it is" or "same ol' same ol'". These are the statements of victims. Yes, that's correct, you are actually victimizing yourself by not using your abilities to the best of your ability.

What we've talked about thus far might seem a lot simpler than it is but most things are. It can be summed up into discovering your desires, making a plan to achieve them and then actually sticking to your plan. For obvious reasons, when simplified this begins to sound like a simple task, but this isn't a project that your doing for someone else. This is as personal as it gets and what that means is that all the attention should rest in the details. We are carving out our space in the world and should attempt to do so with fine detail to assure that the mark we leave is a lasting and impressive one. It is also important to mention not to get too wrongly interpret the word impressive by thinking about others. It is you that you're trying to impress and you that will have to live with whatever result you have created.

Step Three - Enjoying the Moment

Enjoying the moment is of extreme importance because it is something that is often overlooked by some one on a journey. It's very similar to driving somewhere and being so focused on the destination that we forget to actually soak in the scenery and enjoy the moments that got us there. When creating long term goals and visions for ourselves it is easy to either become to engulfed in them or abandon them completely by not taking the tie to enjoy the moment. For me this has become a difficult feat to conquer, especially with the nature of business constantly demanding attention. We have to all find the time to enjoy the moment. When speaking from a financial stand point we have to learn that being focused on the long term does not cancel out our everyday living. We have to learn to include this's in our plans in order to not feel as if we're deviating from the course simply by stopping to smell the roses. Walking down a street that you drive down everyday will unveil a whole new world to you. You now have the time to appreciate the details around you and live in the moment. Learning to do this with your life is a powerful thing to have in your arsenal. This prevents you from losing yourself during the course of your journey.

When adding our desires and constructing our visions we can sometimes forget to include others in the process. This doesn't mean including them in on the actual construction. I'm referring to including the into our thoughts by thinking of how those around us will fit into to our dreams and desires and making sure not to alienate those who care about us in the process. We be so engulfed in our own thought s that we forget to acknowledge the fact that those around us also have their own unique thoughts and ambitions and they have to be able to work together in order for us to work together. When building and acquiring a true oasis we have to remember we eventually want to invite people in. The phrase "Its lonely at the top" is very true, but it doesn't have to be.

The Big Picture

Looking at the big picture can sometimes be a tricky thing to do. Most people assume the best way to do so is to step back to see the entire picture. The truth is there are many ways to look at the big picture and all should be used if given the opportunity. We can step back and soak in the broader aspect of what's being conveyed, or we can move in and look to the details from up close and personal. Neither one of these options should be avoided when looking at the big picture of our lives. We should be looking at it from different angles to gain a better perspective. This might mean attempting to look through someone else's eyes, possibly a loved one, a child, colleague, or even a close associate to help us to know if our visions are infringing on the visions of others. We can also engage in dialogue with others about certain aspects of our visions to gain a new outlook that may even in force us to reevaluate what it is we are looking for out of life. Remember, its the small details that for the big picture.

Jus One

I now want to introduce the concept of both inviting things into and excluding things from our lives. I want to speak about it in less physical terms so that you fully understand the magnitude of what I'm trying to convey. Like most things in life perspective is key. Learning to see the magnitude of the things in our lives will help you to realize the place in our lives things actually belong. This falls directly into the realm of self building and wealth building and provides telescope to look into to see what I refer to as Universal Doors.

Universal Doors

We've all heard the phrase "You have to close one door for another to open". What does this actually mean? It means there simply isn't enough space for everything and our attention cannot be divided into too many different facets before becoming a Jack of all trades and a master of none. The principle of cleaning out our environments to gain clarity and room to invite new and positive circumstances into our lives is also prevalent to opening and closing doors. It may be a negative person in your life that you are spending too much time with. That time can be better spent with someone who is adding a more positive influence on you to aid you while along your journey. That is an example of closing a door. This doesn't mean slam the door, it simply means close it. Its more about realizing that negative influences can and should be escorted to the door. Our inner circles have a capacity similar to that of a club with limited space. For the purpose of this analogy, our individual lives should resemble an exclusive club with people waiting outside to get in. The people we allow into our lives should be those that are willing to contribute to the atmosphere by adding the positivity of their own lives to ours. If we have people inside of the club that are causing disturbances and confusion inside then we have to close the door on them and make room for others to enter. When looking at it from a universal perspective we will see the universe is constantly sending us opportunities that come in the form of people. We have to properly create are oasis in inviting ways to keep them wanting to enter and having the room to be comfortable while doing so.

Before speaking on the benefits of closing doors we should first begin with what prevents us from closing them. I find that the two main things that prevent this from happening is fear and comfortability, and appropriately comfortability of the fear. Many of us spend more time putting up with circumstances rather that creating and controlling them. We put up with things out of the comfortability of dealing with things that we are used to and out of the fear of emptiness. Think about the last time that you've cleaned out your closet. This may be a bad example for those of us with shopping addictions, but ill go out on a limb anyway. Having a closet full of things that we don't wear is certainly not a unique occurrence. Many of us will keep things in the closet out of the same fear of emptiness, yet only when we exhibit true honesty are we able to rid ourselves of all the things that are of no use. Realizing that the only purpose of certain garments is to keep our closets full will help us to clear it out and space for new things to come. What good is having a hundred items in your closet and always flocking to the same ten? Moving that ninety percent out of your closet and out of your life will allow you to properly asses the void. It is in that void that we can clearly see the things that will truly make our life more enriched by bringing in items that we will actually get use and enjoyment out of.

At one point I thought that I'd mastered this concept until one day when I decided to clean out my over cluttered basement and saw all of the things that I had cleared from by closet were packed away in boxes serving absolutely no purpose. The fear of the void was keeping me from feeling confident of fully letting go of things. While cleaning out the basement I couldn't understand why these things were still there. I thought to my my self how many times are you going to throw the same things away. If it wasn't good enough to make the cut and remain in your closet, why is it important enough to be boxed and stored in your basement? This is result of placing things next to the door and feeling like you got rid of it. Ridding yourself of things is a healthy process and so is ridding yourself of circumstances that render you unhappy. Take some time to figure out the things in your life that you have sitting by the door, knowing that the next step is to take it to the curb but are avoiding out of fear and comfortability. What circumstances are we confronted with that we have the ability close the door on to make space for the flow of positive ideas, concepts and people to enter our existence.

How does all of this talk of opening and closing doors fit into the discussion of wealth building? Well actually the stability that comes with maintaining strong finances often produces high levels of fear of change. Closing the door on a job or simply an aspect of your career can prove itself to be much more complicated than one would assume. From the outside looking in it is far easier to utter the words "just quit" without having to pay the bills of the person that actually has to do the quitting.

Fung Shway

This can almost be equivalent to watching a daredevil prepping a stunt and saying "just do it". However, those that care for you and believe in you are never excited about what you debate your greatness. When speaking of our finances in conjunction with our well being we have to delve a little deeper to fully uncover how they can correctly work together. Let's look a little closer into the method of seeing that this happens without driving us crazy in the process.

The Career of Happiness

Is it possible to build a career from happiness? Many times this concept is confused by people who look to find jobs that are fulfilling rather that turning what's fulfilling into a career. By now we've all at one point or another heard that all of us have a unique purpose on earth. We all have talents and interests that should be displayed to add to the world by adding what we have to offer. While in the midst of a career it can become difficult to figure out what makes us happy and we can get lost in the sea of our own ambitions. Looking for work that is self fulfilling can be just as daunting a task as looking for a four leafed clover. The agony of this pursuit can make our work feel even more painful becoming something that we are enduring rather than something we actually enjoy doing. The answer to this type of madness once again comes from within, but it is the technique of discovering it that makes it much easier than we may realize at this point in time. Like many other things we experience and participate in, we have to learn the fundamentals before attempting to expound on them. This is very similar to building a building on a weak foundation. Without a stable foundation, all the decor and designing talents in the world wont be able to take the place of the stability provided by a solid foundation. With this being understood, lets go beneath the surface and discover the technique of building our careers on the foundation of our own happiness.

Monetizing an Emotion:

Monetizing an emotion is the most profitable thing you can do because it not only serves your physical being financially, it also serves your soul in a similar capacity. The act of doing so leans into the way we construct our dreams but it rooted more in what we actually do in the physical world. When asked "What is your talent?" Many of us can be reluctant to answer out of the fear of competing with others that share that particular talent, and many of us simply don't know. For those of us that fall into the unsure category the answer can be found in your interest. Something is drawing you to these specific interest and for a reason. The questions "what do you do" and "what do you do in your spare time" expose the conflict that results in unfulfilling work. The differentiation comes from people that assume that what you do for a living cant be fulfilling enough to be what you do in your spare time and in most cases they are correct.

At a young age I was always impressed by movies where people had made careers from things that they actually enjoy. Whether breakdancing, or surfing, the thought of being so free spirited that you are getting paid to do what you love was in my eyes admirable. The people that were able to live this lifestyle had an extra glow. They appeared to be some of the happiest people on earth and it was the reference point of these people that made conventional jobs so unappealing and draining for me. It lead to believe that the reason they were able to do these things was because they were among the super talented and were lucky to have been discovered and have their talents displayed for a fee. In some cases this was absolutely the case but in many others it couldn't be further from the truth. I began to realize that this phenomenon existed on large and smaller scales all around me, from the florist who loves flowers, to the mechanic who loves cars, people who were doing things before they got paid to do them were much happier than the opposite.

What monetizing an emotion is truly about is asking yourself the latter question of what do you do in your spare time. These actions are where the soul takes you and there are ways to monetize it. Some of us may find ourselves day dreaming about what we consider a hobby but in actuality is a calling. It can range from doodling to the watching of sports or politics. It is all very relevant. we cant allow our selves to think of talents only in a physical sense. Some people have a talent for uncovering the talents of other people. This isn't any less important of a talent than the talents of those they discover. Building a career on these talents might not seem as practical as it sounds, yet, it will always lead to a more fulfilling outcome. Things that make us happy as children can easily reveal to us where the core of our happiness rests. Be it cooking, drawing designing, or simply playing video games, all of the positive emotions that come from these activities have the ability to become monetized.

Now more than ever have the possibilities of gaining capital from the things we love to do become so easily and readily available. With the use of the internet our dreams are now at our fingertips creating room for our hobbies to shoot past our doors into the lives of people around the world making us far more enriched by the things that make us the happiest. Before i allow this to fall into the overflowing category of easier said than done, I'll explain how this is possible to accomplish in a real way to change our lives for the better.

How It's Done:

Step One - Introspection

Introspection is a powerful tool to have in your tool box because it is the key to unlocking your inner self before exposing it to the world. This process may not happen overnight. It takes time to sift through the confusion of what we think we're good at, what we're actually good at, and what actually makes us happy. Sometimes it is a matter of exposure. When we are attempting to monetize what we love we have to learn to explore the entire realm. For instance, if we love something like playing basketball we all know and understand that monetizing something like a sport is what's considered in most cases to be a long shot. How can this help someone who has passed the age of having an opportunity to play professionally? When we explore the entire realm, we will find that there are many different careers associated with playing of basketball. It can range from a personal trainer, to a commentator, to even someone who simply reviews the games online and creates a following from those that are impressed by your passion and understanding of the sport. While you may not possess the talent of Michael Jordan, this will essentially bring you closer to the game you love making it easier for you to find happiness in what it is that you do. It is important during your introspection to explore the entire scope of your desired field to bring you closer to doing what it is you love in ways that are realistic and available to you. I myself began by writing raps and realized my passion for writing music was rooted in writing alone. I realized that the core of my talent was writing and that writing raps was the medium in which I displayed my talent at that particular time. Some of my closest friends were in shock at the sight of my first book, because they didn't correlate the two. Although I had been writing raps in my younger years. I had been writing all along. It was through introspection that I discovered that my passion shouldn't be restricted to one form. After all, if I choose to write a rap today there is nothing stopping me from doing so.

Step Two - Acquiring the tools

Acquiring the tools you need is very simple but extremely important. Don't be afraid to purchase the things you need to get things done. Start simple, don't spend your days daydreaming about things without taking action. After seeing your vision clearly its time to feel. Now its time to touch your dream by pulling it into the physical world with us. This doesn't mean you have to go broke i the process. It simply means take the leap. There's nothing wrong with using preowned equipment and you shouldn't hesitate to get your hands on what you need. While we understand the power we can harness from our dreams, we must also understand some batteries can be destroyed by leaving them on the charger for too long. Spending all of our time dreaming about something is the same as leaving something on the charger for prolonged periods of time. The outlet is very powerful, but things are charged up so they can be of use. Make sure you don't over exert your battery with out getting use out of the charge. Something key to remember is, never look at the objects that support your vision as if they are toys or something that you are undeserving of. The truth is it wouldn't matter if it were literal toys that you required to see your vision thru. You may find yourself unboxing toys and reviewing them, or trading rare toys online. The possibilities are limitless and the choice is yours as to what will make you happy. Its not for others to decide or have anything more than an opinion on, unless it is something that may cause harm or lead to your detriment. assuming you're intentions are positive in nature, those who are around you and involved in your life should also get excited at seeing your visions turn into a reality.

Step Three - Belief & Commitment

Believing that what it is your doing is a part of yourself, you will better understand how the things you are doing is you being yourself. Having the necessary tools to hone your craft will only help you to further believe in yourself and commit to what it is your doing. You have to dive into your craft as if it were a job because this is what will free your from your job. Its only fair for me to acknowledge that there is absolutely no guarantee that you will successfully transition yourself into the career of your dreams. However, it is our duty to except the opportunity to attempt to free ourselves whole heartedly. This commitment that you make, with the proper amount of balance can only benefit you. Either you become successful at what you love, or you spend your free time enjoying it and find happiness in the balance and productivity. There is no loss in this situation. Believe in yourself and commit to expanding on your talents and passions and the energy created will be positive in nature.

Step Four - Sharing

Wear your passions with pride. Make bold declarations to let others know who and what you are. By affirming yourself with others this will add to the power you possess by creating more energy. It will transcend past your own belief into others belief in you. This is what brings things into existence. Don't confuse this with seeking validation. We should not be concerned with the validation of those that don't precede us in our desired field. However, sharing does require objectivity. We can't allow our passion for something to always transfer into a talent for something. This is the purpose of exploring all aspects associated with vision we've created. By the way this is not at all to be confused with some "fake it till you make it" type of hustle. Its simple about affirming what you are to yourself and the world. Its the action that allows you to speak out honestly about yourself while solidifying your own reality. If you make hats, the moment you finish your second hat you gone from someone who made a hat to someone that now makes "hat's". The same goes for paintings sculptures, baked goods etc. This isn't about cheating or embellishing. This is about the power that comes from action and our use of that power. If you love doing something that is positive affirm it. Take great pride in the side of yourself that you display to the world and your talents should be at the forefront.

Summary

The bottom line (no pun intended) is that there are huge correlations between self building and wealth building. The two actually go hand in hand. We must remove the stigma associated with spirituality and material things. Getting in touch with our ambitions is a very spiritual process that when the proper efforts are applied leads to a physical or material result. Absent the issue of overindulging, assuming we all understand the difference between what's realistic and what's not, we will learn that in terms of our inner visions our wants are our needs. I'll say that one again because I really want you to understand this statement that most likely goes against what most of us have been taught for our entire lives. That's correct, our wants are our needs. The fact is your wants are the real you speaking and what drives your physical being in certain directions and in that regard denying yourself is depriving yourself. Our being consists of many different facets and finance happens to be a part of it. Whether building a career from happiness of finding happiness in a career, the true purpose is to build self so that you can exhibit your true potential for the world to enjoy

Chapter Seven
Relationship Diagnostics

No matter how introverted one might be, we all engage in relationships. It is up to us to discover if these relationships are healthy or destructive. Sometimes we will find ourselves in situations that are helpful to others, but detrimental to ourselves. In life one unaddressed issues may surely lead to another issue. This process is very similar to the maintenance of a vehicle and we will explore it in a similar fashion. Our vehicles and our relationships are equipped with sensors and warning signals to keep us aware of what may be wrong at any given time. These sensors and signals can be further explored by the use of diagnostics. Your diagnostics will run a series of tests to find the root of a problem giving you the chance to zero in on what's affecting your vehicle negatively.

Ironically, we will be comparing our physical existence in this life to a vehicle, which is exactly what our physical existence consists of. This is not only about the relationships that surround us, its also about the most important relationship of all, the one between vehicle and driver. After all, the driver and vehicle's relationship must be a balanced one because both are needed to sustain each other and that is the true definition of a relationship. Some people believe that as long as the wheels are rolling the car is fine, but the reality is that there can be many existing issues that may actually lead you directly into danger. That's right, you may be driving yourselves crazy, or even worse driving yourself to your own destruction. Without further delay lets roll up our sleeves and pop the hood to take a look at the status of our vehicle and strengthen our relationship with it in the process.

Assessment

We should begin by taking a deeper look not the functioning of our vehicle to get a better sense of if it is working in our best interest. Relationships in our lives require this type of look for the very same reasons. The most important aspect of our vehicle is its reliability. No one is looking for a vehicle that requires more than a moderate amount of maintenance. The difference between vehicles and relationships is that vehicles don't heal over time. If you park it without fixing it, no amount of time will permit a healing process to occur. The problems of a vehicle will remain and without intervention if not parked will affect the functionality of other parts of your vehicle and this function is very similar to the way our relationships work. When we allow problems to fester without being addressed they will put a strain on other aspects of our lives. On the dashboard of our cars we can find lights that illuminate when a particular function of our car isn't working properly. Similarly, our lives have red flags that will avail themselves to us at different times to help us keep our lives in the best condition.

Let's begin by discussing the basic needs of our vehicles and relationships and how they affect the experiences we have with them. First, let's take a look at some of the simple things, then gradually move on to a more complex diagnostic of our vehicles.

Gas and Fluids

Have you ever noticed that cars seem to run better when they have a decent amount of gas? Run your car on empty puts a strain on other parts that may not be visible, but is negatively affecting your drive. We all suffer from different financial difficulties at times in our lives. However, the sole purpose of a car is to drive and that function is not possible without gas. Gas in terms of our relationships is what drives us. It's what keeps us interacting with the people we interact with, the reason for doing so. Some of our relationships may be running out of gas. It is our option, to refuel or to allow the relationship to simply run its course. Are our relationships running out of gas? This is an important question to ask ourselves. If so, are we interested in refueling them or are we looking to let someone else take over the payments or possibly even watch the relationship hauled off to the junkyard while you smile in the backdrop? The most significant thing to remember is that the choice is always yours. We don't have to continually refuel relationships that have lost their drive. When the vehicle has lost its drive, the decision to continue lies solely on the driver. It must be noted that if you choose to continue, it will require action.

The Oil Change

The oil change is a vital part of keeping our vehicles in the right condition to drive. If you are interested in keeping your vehicle running smoothly the oil change is routine action that encompasses much more than simply changing your oil. During this process all of the fluids that run throughout your car will be checked and "topped off" to get you through the next part of your journey. The oil is what keeps the relationship working quietly, free of noise and complaints. Making sure the oil is clean and fresh is a part of care for your car. The oil in our relationships lies with what our relationships are based on. Whether business or personal, they all have something that keeps them running smoothly. Its a principle part of our relationships to stop every so often to make sure that the oil that runs through our situation has become toxic, because just as the fresh oil flows through the entire system, the toxic oil will do the same, only this will be a corrupting and polluting force that will undoubtedly impact our situations negatively.

Turn Down the Radio

At some point we all like to blast our favorite song while cruising down the highway, but it's important to remember that the the distress sounds of our cars need to be available to our ears. Think about a lifeguard that sits on his post blasting music in his earbuds. Yes, the feeling of flying down the highway or sitting next to the ocean blasting music that seems to fit the moment like a glove is more than appealing. However, we must remain aware of our surroundings and be responsible for the outcomes of the events around us. When it comes to our relationships, we should acknowledge that when people speak we should be listening, whether we agree or not. Allowing others to voice their grievances, concerns, or feelings on a deaf ear is nothing short of selective hearing, which is no different that turning up the music in your car to avoid hearing the sounds your car is making alerting you to a problem occurring with your vehicle. There is a stark difference between assessing what you hear and choosing what you hear. We have to learn to place things in there proper category after hearing them rather than pretending that we didn't heat them at all when in regards to our relationships. Does a falling tree in the forest make a sound if no one is there to hear it? The answer is yes, its the ego of man that would question this. When the people around us make sounds its best to not pretend that we weren't there to hear it if we want the relationship to survive.

Don't Ignore the Lights

What is it that make us ignore the lights? While there are some of you reading this thinking how trivial this may be, try to understand that there is a large population of us that will ignore the lights and warning signals displayed for a variety of reasons. These reasons can range from fear of cost to utter negligence, but all will have the same result. Why is it that we don't ignore the traffic lights? Well, most likely is because we all understand the dangers that can occur from doing so and the instant ramifications that might possibly follow. We have to understand that knowing the problem doesn't meant that we will be able to fix it but it certainly increases our chances. When we have know idea of what's going on and ignore the warning signs provided, we have entered dangerous water where the chance of being rescued are very slim. Think about it, if you were at sea would you ignore the flare gun blasted in sky for all to sea? Wouldn't a rational person be interested in discovering what was going on and if they're going to be effected by it? The light on or dashboard work in a similar capacity. They alert us to problems that may effect us and are simply not to be ignored. Turning a blind eye to these lights will not make your ride smoother in any way. In fact, they will begin to lay in your subconscious mind. This will make you want to drive your vehicle less and it will slowly begin to not serve the purpose intended. This is the purpose and importance of running diagnostics tests. It will free you from placing problems in your subconscious mind and make it easier to address them to keep your ride smooth and enjoyable.

Vehicle and Relationship Types

Let's be honest, all relationships and vehicles are not the same and won't be cared for and treated in the same way either. Identifying the different types of relationships and vehicle helps us to honestly address wha each vehicle type would need to remain functional. While in some cases the "treat everyone the same" mentality works, its not applicable in all situations. It's not realistic to think that people will treat a complete stranger in the same way that they will treat a loved one, just as you wouldn't treat a brand new luxury car the same way way you'd treat an old car with fifteen previous owners. The phrase "treat everyone how you would like to be treated" needs to be looked at from another angle before we proceed our exploration of these relationships.

When we look at the that particular phrase we need to understand that treating others the way we would like to be treated is in the best interest of everyone, but the position they are in does apply. We would all like to be treated like a king or a queen in all of our endeavors. What we have to realize is that we have to look at the position first. It doesn't mean that we are to treat everyone as royalty. What it suggest is that you treat the king with the respect that you would want as a king and treat the lower level employee how you would like to be treated as a lower level employee. Sounds simple enough, yet many of us are find ourselves addicted to the feeling of being exalted and projecting that feeling onto those we feel we can get away with this type of behavior. Now that we understand that there are clearly different types of relationships, lets take a look at the different ways we can approach and care for them.

Family: The Bentley

When you purchase a luxury car of this type you have to factor in the cost of maintenance and repair. It isn't at all wise to buy this type of car until you can afford all that comes with it. The cost of this vehicle doesn't mean that it is void of problems. It means that the luxury the car provides requires a higher caliber of repair when something goes wrong because the car is extremely high in value. Our relationships with our family are extremely high in value and are very similar to the comfort of a luxury vehicle. When a conflict arises with a member of our family the cost of repair can be high because it requires more care and attention than others. When damage occurs to these relationships the hurt that comes with it requires the utmost attention because it attacks the luxury and comfort provided in our sacred space. Holding our family members in high esteem by placing them at Bentley status makes it easier to maintain these relationships the way that they need to be treated. The family structure is by far the most valuable asset one can have yet it does require care. All of the different types of care that we've previously discussed apply to our family vehicle at the highest level. We should never ignore the lights and waning signs on the dashboard of this vehicle. This is an immediate pull over or head straight to the mechanic situation to ensure that our family vehicle is running as strong and smoothly as possible. When a problem surfaces, remember the comforting luxury of your family as riding in your Bentley on the sunniest day playing your favorite song and make sure you remedy the situation as swiftly as possible to get you back to your desired state of luxury.

Friends: The Mercedes Benz

Our friends also fall into the status of luxury. In this lifetime we all understand that friends may walk in and out of our lives. However, the time spent them is in every way a luxury experience. When we begin to treat our friends as "just a friend" and dis regard the luxury provided fro them we are trivializing what they are giving us and in some ways becoming unworthy of receiving this pleasure. Friends of ours are extremely valuable assets in this lifetime. Often we overlook them and take advantage of the close relationship with them by not providing the necessary care for them. A lot of times we don't respect the value of something or someone until either a problem surfaces or the person walks out out of our lives. Since we have been speaking about vehicles the words "hindsight is always twenty/twenty" becomes more apparent and applicable. What this means is that what's in the rear view mirror always appears more clearly than what's in front of us because it is rooted in retrospect and allows reflection. It is always easier to say what we could have and should have done, especially when we are speaking about something that is high in value. It's important understand what we have when we have it. That's the only way to properly care for it and ensure that it works for us and is compatible with us. Sometimes we get frustrated with the functionality of something because we don't understand its purpose. When this happens things normally go in the wrong direction because we expect from our vehicle what it is not intended to provide. We should at first know ourselves as drivers before driving, but we should also know the vehicle we are driving as well. This way you won't be trying to take your new sedan off road and finding yourself devaluing the relationship between you and your vehicle.

Love Interest: The Mercedes Benz Coupe

The love interest or the coupe as I choose to call it is also an important vehicle that requires a different level of care. This is not to be confused with shopping on the car lot or simply dating. This is the lease with the option to buy. When you are considering the buy option you care for the vehicle as if it were your own before the actual purchase. You tend to its needs in a way that is similar to the similar to the way we treat our friends. This vehicle is a two seater for obvious reasons, it is about you and your love interest alone and how the two of you function together. This is an important vehicle because it represents a person you might possibly be bringing into the fold of friends and family. This is something you are looking to withstand the test of time and requires care and focus to achieve the desired result. This particular vehicle is unique because it comes with upgrade options to possibly becoming a Bentley coupe, meaning one day becoming a member of your family. Although the other family vehicles on your lot may have more of a solidified spot, they will all understand the position of the Mercedes coupe and welcome it onto the lot depending the relationship you have with it. The way they see you care for this car in comparison to the way the car drives for you does matter. It is a very important aspect of how comfortable this car will be while parked in the stable of your other luxury vehicles. The nature of a two seater vehicle is very personal, however it must be understood that there are other vehicles that also require attention. Beware of the two seater that wants to be the only car on your lot, or you will find yourself losing some extremely valuable vehicles in the process.

Business: The Town Car

The town car may not be the most luxurious vehicle you own it does require a degree of detailing to remain respectable. What this means is that while others will understand that you are the owner of several luxury vehicles that you care for mor than this one, they want to see you while driving this vehicle treating it as if its your only one. This is the vehicle that others will understand if miss a car wash due to attending to one of your other vehicles. However, this cannot become a habit. The town car will remain a nice car that does not mind being parked amongst luxury vehicles but will not stand for constant neglect. It knows and understands its value and position and will position itself where it will be of the best use and cared for properly. In a perfect world we would all be able to drive nothing luxury vehicles all day and every day, but for most of us we need to have a reliable vehicle capable of doing more driving than these other vehicles are capable of. This vehicle is similar to the coupe regarding the delicate nature of the amount of time spent with it. It requires a delicate balance of time delegation to ensure that it is not being overused or underused. It should always remain in top condition because the reliability of this vehicle is what creates the room for the luxury of the others.

Everyone Else: The Bucket

You may or may not own a bucket, after all it represents the most expendable of all vehicles. These are the vehicles you see around you everyday and don't meant enough to you to want own or purchase. However, these vehicles a vast and the fact of the matter is that they all cannot be classified as junk. In fact, some of the ones you come in contact with a the luxury vehicles of others. They are to be treated with respect and not ignored. While it is not your job to maintain the upkeep of said vehicle, it should be understood that someone else does care for this vehicle in the way that yo care for the luxury cars in your garage. The light on the dashboards of these vehicles is not your concern, but lending a helping hand to someone in need should never be completely removed from the spectrum. When we keep in our minds that the value of these vehicles may be greater to others we will understandably show the respect for that them that we desire for our own vehicles and hopefully that respect is reciprocated properly back to us during the course of our lives. It's not a logical perspective to think that you should care for these vehicles in the same way you care for your own. However, care and respect are two very different things and all vehicles whether parked or on the road deserve some level of respect. It is this level of respect that makes it easier to maintain our own vehicles because it simple makes the world easier to function in if everyone shares some level of respect for one another.

The Diagnostics Test

Now that we've discussed some of the different forms of maintenance and vehicle types, lets take a look at running an actual diagnostics test to keep our vehicles running in the best condition possible. Below you find some diagnostics information for the relationships that we are engaged in that may reshape our entire diving experience for the better. Without further delay let's plug these vehicles up and see what we're working with.

Running the Test

The Oil Light: The oil of the car is very important in making sure our vehicle runs at its top performance level. Not only is the oils level necessary to be maintained, but also the oil must be changed to ensure that we are not running dirty fluids through our cars. This translates into our relationships in the very same way. We have to understand that what keeps our situations fresh is clean communication. Being dishonest or caging our feelings sends fluid throughout our situations but that fluid is dirty and can actually damage or vehicles engine. The communication that happens between the people closest to us should always remain clean in order to ensure that the engine is running at its highest capacity. Honesty is that clean oil. In the real world things will be said and situations will occur, but its critical that we take pit stops to clean our oil to make sure that the overtone of our situations is positive. If you become known as a liar, or someone that is in the habit of stretching or caging the truth, the relationships around you will eventually become toxic due to the fluid that you are pumping through them. Take time to asses your oil and make sure to change it as often as you should. It will make a much better driving experience for you in your travels.

The Engine Light: The engine light is perhaps the most important of all of the lights on our dashboard. It is literally the foundation of the entire vehicle. This goes far beyond the cosmetic viewpoint that most of us are normally accustomed to. The engine is fundamentally the entire car or relationship. This represents more than a problem brewing. If this particular light is not addressed the relationship may not survive. The fact of the matter is that even if this is addressed the relationship may not survive. This is the light that signals that it may not be possible for the relationship to move further. Engine trouble signals an immediate pull over situation. However, it's important to remember this doesn't signal the end of the road for this vehicle. Just like a car, relationships have different parts and components. The engine may be a critical part of our vehicle, but even the engine breaks into parts. Every concern that relates to the engine is pivotal but does not elude to the end. It represents extreme concerns that we should be aware of and address immediately.

The Transmission Light: The transmission represents how our relationships flow. It is how we change gears both figuratively and literally. Change will occur in everything we do in life. Change can effect us negatively or positively depending on how we respond to that change. It may be a change in career or the career of someone close to us, or possibly a significant other that has chosen to move on. Either way, this change must be responded to in order to ensure that thing will flow correctly into the next progression or stage in your relationship. This in essence is a shift in gears. The fluid that makes the transmission operate in our relationships is communication. We have to be aware of the goals of those who surround us so. That the changes that occurs in their lives are celebrated by us all or aided if necessary. Be mindful of the the situations and life decisions of others around us because they may ultimately impact our lives in the process.

Summary

The bottom line is that in order to enjoy the people around us in a way that is deserving to us all we will have to implement some degree of work. Before the actually work comes into play we have to care and care is something that has been underrated in this day and time. Love is in some ways an uncontrollable force that takes over the mind and body, while care on the other hand requires action. Care leads to caring and caring is an action. It's where your mind and body connect for the betterment of someone other than yourself. People that care for us should be held in the highest regard and we should remember that everyone around us is cared for by someone else. When we properly care for the people that have important roles in our lives the maintenance can be an enjoyable experience. It doesn't have to be considered "work" with a negative connotation deeming it something grueling and painstaking. When we begin to feel this way we need to decide if this particular vehicle is for us or if we need to place it in the shop for a major repair no matter the cost. It's better to be honest rather than disingenuous and run the risk of losing our vehicle along with the time we've previously invested in it. Life itself can create some undesirable road conditions but this doesn't mean driving our vehicles has to be a "strap on your seatbelt, it going to be a bumpy ride" type of situation. Knowing, understanding and caring for your vehicle will help it last a lifetime.

Chapter Eight
Consciousness

Consciousness: The state of being awake and aware of one's surroundings.

I f Feng Shui relies on the placement of things in order to allow the correct types of energy to flow, then it is an appropriate assertion that consciousness is paramount to achieving our intended outcome. The state of being awake and aware of our surroundings can go much further than our present mind can comprehend at this present time. When we think about our surroundings, we tend to only focus on our immediate surroundings of what we can see. If you asked someone to describe their surroundings, they will most likely describe the room they're in or the street, they're walking on and would not be wrong in doing so. When we begin to open our minds, we understand that our surroundings are as vast as the ever expanding universe. Before continuing I'd like to explain that I don't mean any of this in a spooky sense. However, it is important for this type of study to understand that some things they we may deem a little weird might actually have a place understanding who and what we are. After all, I think it's fair to say the concept of life itself is a little strange and weird in the fact that we all are wondering what is actually going on struggling to find purpose. While those of us who have seemed to master this physical existence by acquiring the material possessions they set out to impress us in their mastery, we will find that that there is a lot left to be desired. This is the balance that we look for that is often abandoned during our earthly experiences. You will find that most of us choose sides in where our focus lies. When people are engaged in the rat race or paper chase, they will find themselves less connected to the other side of themselves, which isn't necessarily a bad thing. It's the balance that makes everything make sense. Allow me to explain in detail how balance plays a major role in our being.

Balance: Life on the Seesaw

In an ever expanding universe we must all realize that it could not exist without balance. Some refer to it as Yin and Yang, right and wrong, negative and positive, or even left and right. This infers is that there will always be the existence of polarity, but with polarity sometimes comes sacrifice. When we go right, we sacrifice what's available to us on the left. Our lives are full of these compromises. They surface in the form of decisions. The decisions we make are what shape our lives. The life we end up with is a result of the decisions we've made be they good or bad. In order to keep a balance we must remain awake and aware of our surroundings, which is the state of consciousness. We may choose to be solely focused on our financial gain and in the process neglect everything around us that does not support that particular goal. Adversely, we may focus on the feelings of others and our mental growth and end up not being able to pay a bill. This doesn't mean that we are spending our time in the wrong way, but we do have to acknowledge the sacrifice being made so that we can fully comprehend the road we are traveling. When we acknowledge a particular sacrifice it makes our decision making process a little more clear and concise. When we disregard the fact that we are making these sacrifices it leaves room for us to place blame on others for the decisions we've made in our own lives. Every choice we make comes with the sacrifice of another choice. This is the balance that the universe consists of. There is no riding of the fence as far as the universe is concerned. Living with this particular understanding requires learning to live with regrets. Your moral compass is what determines the degree of regret you will have to deal with in certain scenarios that involve a moral decision as a part of your process. We have to find ways of keeping a balance between moral and practical to remain on a level playing field. After all, level spelled backwards is level and this should serve as the perfect reminder of keeping balance in our lives.

Right vs Left

In an ever expanding universe what exactly is up and down, left or right, in or out? Does it really exist? If left and right is infinite and up and down is as well, do these directions really exist? On a large scale I would have to say no. However, when we break these things down to smaller levels I find that they are merely used as navigation points. On this plane of existence we need to have a mental and moral compass that we use to guide our decision making process while on our course. This directly relates to the seesaw that we've just spoken of. We as humans don't have to fully comprehend how the seesaw works, but understanding that it exists is what make humans truly unique. This understanding creates a build or destroy effect in the world around us. When we hear the words build and destroy we tend to think in terms of negative and positive, but this isn't always the case. Building and destroying can work in an infinite amount of ways. When we build a new structure we have destroyed the previous scenery but that doesn't necessarily indicate a bad thing. Good and bad are merely an outcome of perception. This is not meant in a sociopathic way to justify heinous or criminal acts that are apparently bad. I'm referring to the way that look at situations to remain aware of the ripples they may cause in the waters around us. What is good for us may not be good for others. Our perception is often dictated by our place in the world. For instance, lets take a look at a famous fictional character by the name of Robin Hood to gain a better perspective of how perspective works.

Outside of Self

In this existence we must learn to not become consumed with self. When we do we will forget to understand the existence of others around us. Looking at the world can only be done from our own eyes but sometimes we must do our best to remember that the people that exist outside of ourselves see us in the same way that we see them, as someone outside of ourselves. When we start to believe that the world belongs to us and our perspective we do ourselves and the world a disservice. There are moments when we have to be selfish and there are also moments that require us to step outside of ourselves to create the right balance to coexist in the world with others. This phenomenon is what's known as the proper gesture. What this means is that at any given moment there is a proper way of handling a situation and equally a proper thing to say.

This prevents the convolution that comes from handling things improperly. We know that we will never be able to see from any eyes other than our own, but at times attempting to due so is the proper gesture.

Consciousness: The Awareness or Perception of Something by a Person.

This particular aspect of consciousness deals with an aspect of our being that can change at any time but is also as unique as our very own finger print, our perspective. The perspective that we hold is unique due to no one being able to see from the exact same viewpoint. Science won't allow two objects to occupy the same space and time. Therefore it will be impossible for someone to see exactly what you see at the exact same time as you. Something will remain completely unique to their perspective. This doesn't change the fact that we will share similar views with those around us or others in the world. What it does mean is that that we cant expect the opinions of others to always reflect the ones we have. Remembering this fact is what keeps us balanced and helps to refrain us from forcing our opinions onto those who cannot see from our perspective.

Many political and religious discussions end in anger and dissent due to those that feel everyone should share their perspective. A view can can only be explained and expounded on. Attempting to force a view into the eyes of someone else will prove itself to be a daunting and difficult task that will only make a fool out of the one doing the forcing. The life experiences that we've accumulated over time create our reality of the world. Sometimes its necessary to take this into account when trying to communicate ideas to others. Perhaps you should start by explaining your viewpoint to others to give them a frame of reference to understand where your coming from. Would you expect a sports writer to be able to write a sci-fi film on request? It wouldn't exactly be the most reasonable thing to ask for due to their frame of reference and life experiences. However, if we knew that this sports writer was an avid fan of sci-fi and spent every free moment they had away from the wide world of sports watching these types of films, it would certainly impact the decision to ask them to do such a thing. Speaking with people and communicating with them is one step to understanding them. The other is to try see where they're coming from in order to gain perspective on why the see the world the way the world the way the do to create a better cohesion between the parties involved, which will almost certainly render a better outcome.

Robin Hood

When we think of the story of Robin Hood we tend to discard all of his political motives and sum his story up to one phrase, "robbing from the rich and giving to the poor". Many political and socioeconomic debates have referenced this one particular aspect of his story. Morally, we can all agree that robbing is wrong. However, someone that is known for the act of robbing others has managed to become a hero of sorts, even having his criminal acts glorified in children's books world over. This is how perception works. It allows us to make decisions on the things we see and come up with our own conclusions to what we've witnessed by making decisions and sacrifices. Let's dive right in to the debate by asking this question. Is Robin Hood a good guy or a bad guy? In all fairness, with the exception of unforgivable acts such as murders, rapes, molestation etc, judging someone on a scale of good and bad based off of one act isn't the easiest thing to do. This is one of the reasons why juries exist. Judging requires different perceptions and perspectives and even then will still be subject to error. However, its the act of judgment that is the root of this particular discussion and that's what should be focused on at the moment. Understanding perception helps us to recognize the need for communication. When we realize that everyone may not share our perspective due to their own perception of things it strengthens our communication skills to properly convey our messages to the world.

Vision vs Visualize

The major difference between vision and visualizing is control. Having vision or more specifically, a vision doesn't require control. It's the act of visualizing that requires the control we have latent in our potential. Vision itself can come at any time without our consent, hence the bright idea. The fact that this is true doesn't mean that one should hold more value than the other. It simply means they are different and we are choosing to recognize that difference to make our lives better by acknowledging what's true in the world we live in. Lets take a look at this phenomenon in a little more detail to again explore some truths that can potentially better our lives and the lives of those around us.

Many ancient societies have given reverence to the presence of visions, one in particular are the Native Americans. This culture has a practice that is known as a vision quest where people go off on a quest in hopes of having a vision that would steer them in the correct direction for their careers by finding purpose in life. This vision comes by way of entering a sweat lodge without indulging in food or drink for a period of time and experiencing a form of hallucination that they wouldn't have otherwise encountered. This is an action that separates the vision from visualizing. In the world we live in we often find ourselves trapped in cycles that make it extremely difficult to find the time to create an independent thought. This practice is what's known as meditation. Most people don't find ways to incorporate meditation into their daily lives. In some instances its because we don't see it as something worth prioritizing and in other cases we don't understand the benefits from doing so. Lets take the concept of vacation for example. There are some of us that see vacationing as simply traveling and having a good time, which is good for our physical being as well as our mental state. Adversely, there are others that feel that they absolutely need to take a vacation to free their minds from the daily activities that the are engulfed in on a regular basis. The truth is that both are right. Traveling and having a good time is both fun as well as necessary. The part of this that often flies over people's heads is that the benefits of vacationing should be experienced daily. There is a large segment of people that feel that meditation takes too much time and isn't realistic to attempt daily, thus making them abandon the practice entirely. For that I will say, meditation is a private practice. The time limit is set by you. All it means is that at some point of everyday you should have time for yourself. Time for yourself to acknowledge yourself, not your favorite show, or your favorite song, or even sleep, but rather time to spend developing a clear thought during your waking hours to help center yourself. Whether one minute or one hour we all need time for our minds to vacation from the lives that we live physically every day. This focus often helps us physically because it is certainly true that where the mind goes the body will follow.

Consciousnesses: The Fact of Awareness by the Mind of Itself and the World.

People often associate the word consciousness to being aware of something. The problem with this is that we have to acknowledge that everyone is aware of something. What we should take into account is that while we all live in the same world together, we may not live in the same dynamic as others. At a base level we can all agree that we share the very same breath of life. We are all living beings that are sharing an earthly experience. From the moment of inception consciousness exists. Our consciousness expands with the information and experiences that we undergo in our lifetime. Unfortunately in that the same regard the knowledge of ourselves should also greatly increase during the course of our lives, but seems to become lost as we become overwhelmed with what happens outside of ourselves. Learning ourselves and learning the world we live in can go hand in hand. If our goal is to better the world by bettering ourselves the first step is to understand yourself. How can we attempt to better what we don't understand? The first initial step in bettering ourselves is recognize our existence in the world and the presence of our being in our own bodies. Although this discovery sometimes proves a little difficult at root, its actually a very simple concept that can be acknowledged even simpler. All that has to be done is saying to yourself "I am a living being and a part of the world I live in". The thoughts that come after that are the details of your existence and those thoughts take time to process.

Existence

When speaking about a broad topic such as existence it's important to remember that every thing in existence has the right to exist and every living thing will fight for their own existence. It is not the existence of negativity that is the problem, but rather forcing it on others or having it forced on you that creates problems and impedes progress. From the initial existence of human beings I'm almost certain the question of why we exist was there. Maybe the answer was there and somehow was lost in translation or maybe it was never there at all, but throughout my existence I've come to find that the answer that is most helpful to me is that things exist because hey do. Some soul searchers may not at all satisfied with that but its their right not to be. That creates another perspective and in turn another existence. In this life we will do better searching for what to do with our existence as opposed to searching for why we exist in the first place. What would come from a painter that sat in a room with paint supplies and an empty canvas pondering why they exist, or why paint at all? At that moment a better question would be "what should I paint" to make things actually manifest on our limited time on this earth. There is nothing wrong with questioning our existence, however, bringing things into existence will better serve us and the word around you.

The Real in Reality

Let's take a second to separate what's real from reality. Reality is supposed to represent all that is real in the world compiled into one dynamic. However, reality for some doesn't always consist of what's real. In many instances there are those that create their own reality from what they simply wish to be true. How is it possible to create a reality? If reality is supposed to consist of what's actually real, how is it possible to create a false reality? Actually, that would be an oxymoron that we have chosen to adapt to for reasons of comfort. Acknowledging and separating what's actually real is an extremely powerful thing to do. This is the equivalent of playing with a common toy intended for toddlers where the object is to place a peg with a specific shape into the space that fits. The problem with forcing a false reality is it only exist in theory or if gone unchallenged. This is in essence trying to force the square peg into the space designated for the circle. In order to solve any problem, especially ones related to our existence we have to separate what is real from what we believe to be our reality.

One thing that seems to convolute this issue is emotionalism. First off, this isn't intended to devalue our emotions or even question their significance. It means that when entering the realm of problem solving we have to be able to separate them from issues and put them in their proper place. Our emotions are the warning signs of problems that exist. However, they are not the actual problem. Individuals spend too much time focusing on how a problem feel rather than addressing the problem itself and allowing the feeling to change. This occurs on both sides of the spectrum. If something makes us feel good we will ignore what's true about the situation to keep the feeling alive and the same occurs with a bad feeling, we will ignore the truth about the situation in order to focus on what's inherently negative about the ordeal. Learning how to recognize the validity of our emotions and separate them from what's real is what shapes our reality in the correct way. The only way to properly address an issue and find resolve is to firmly root yourself in the truth and that is to differentiate what's real from reality.

The United States of Being

Our mental states in the different facets of our mind combined with the state of our physical being is what I like to call The United States of Being. This I what's referred to with the general question that we either ask someone every day, or are asked by someone everyday, "How are you doing?" The question itself is simple enough, but it speaks directly to the entirety of our lives. If someone were to ask you this question, it is in most cases apparent that they are not asking for an itemized description of your life, but rather an overall assessment of your state of being. The United States of your being should be taken into consideration when assessing your own life. However, just like government, many of the problems that exist inside of you individually at state level. Now, with all things considered ask yourselves this question "How are you doing?"

Chapter Nine
The Journey Continues

We are now approaching the end of the ride and should certainly be feeling much more invigorated than when we initially started. We should be much more organized and if applied correctly positive energy should already have begun to flow through your life and begin to start manifesting more positivity in your lives. Again, this is not a book of magic, but it certainly can be a magical book. The results we will achieve when applying the principles in this book can spawn a positive field of energy over our lives and the lives of those around us. Be sure to take the time to observe not only how things are working for you by reassessing the perception of yourself. When your perception of yourself and your current state of being grows and develops into fondness the perception others have of you will also grow into fondness. The fondness of yourself is most important because it lights the fire of confidence that attracts others to that particular energy. This is the point where you have become your own greatest inspiration because you are now inspiring others to achieve e greatness. The greatness that you have sought after has infused itself with the unique qualities of your making you an example of greatness for those around you to aspire to. We are in essence, learning how to walk again. Just as we learned how to walk in our infant stages, it wasn't the process that we focused on, but merely the desire to reach our destination. Now we understand the process of processing, which gives us the luxury and liberty of observation on the road traveled and this is truly the living experience. With our newfound understanding of our existence, let's explore a few more concepts before bringing our journey full circle.

Expansion

Let's take a look at the dynamic of expansion. For many, there is a common belief that bigger is better. However, most rational people will not exclude the existence of quality being a factor in determining what is best. With this understanding we can look further into the concept of expansion. When it comes to our minds, the bigger the better. We have to be able to think as vast as the universe offers to not become bound to one spot and stuck in a rut of sorts in the process. The art of Feng Shui involves the placement of objects in certain positions to create balance, allowing the proper flow of energy to exist within a space. What this means in terms of expansion is removing or repositioning things in our mental reservoir creates more space and helps to expand our thoughts more clearly. Think about your personal computer screen and imagine that you have everything that you've done on this computer scattered all over the desktop. This clutter is what prevents you from adding more or even understanding what you already have there. In this same regard, we need to commit these entries to folders in order to organize them and create more space for us to add more things and control our thoughts. Similar to the computer, we also have a limited amount of space, but organizing gives the appearance of more allowing us to not exclude valuable information due to useless data we had stored previously. Anyone who has rushed to their phone to take a picture in the heat of the moment and was stifled by not having enough room in the phone to take the picture knows exactly what I'm speaking about. The information that we store has to be processed, filed and in some cases thrown in the trash can. Let's take this opportunity to look at how we can apply this in our own lives to create a clear and balanced mind, free of confining clutter.

The topics discussed in this book were designed to take our major thoughts and give us the ability to organize them without attempting to micromanage what's personal to our own lives. We have to use our own discretion in most facets of our adult lives, especially when it comes to the prioritizing of our lives. Whether we are predominately serious or predominantly goofy we all have to create the proper balance to not fall off the edge of one particular side. This doesn't mean that someone who is serious by nature should attempt to become equally as goofy and destroy who they innately are. It means that in order to strengthen yourself you should expose yourself to what you enjoy and resonate with and also expose yourselves while occasionally exposing yourselves to things that you have no knowledge of in order to experience something new that you may find enjoyable. In other words, if you have a favorite sports team don't spend most of your time watching the team that you hate. It creates negative energy that you may not realize that you are storing and lugging around with you. In the same vein be careful not to spend all of your time watching the one team that you love. If you truly enjoy the sport you will be cutting yourself off from the opportunity of seeing what other teams have to offer. This same principle applies to many different things in our lives, particularly things that we may find difficult to step out of our comfort zones and allow a different perspective to invade our sacred spaces. Whether politics, religion or even the people that we engage with in our lives the same principle applies. For instance, we can watch the news channel that we tend to agree with predominantly to prevent us from spending our evenings yelling at the television at people that aren't listening, but from time to time we have to be able to listen to the opposing argument presented by another station. The same theory should apply to religion. If you're confident in what you subscribe to you should have no problem occasionally consorting with an alternative view. What gives you the ability to posses this type of confidence is the processing of thoughts. If you've truly processed the thoughts that you've acquired as opposed to simply being indoctrinated and programmed then you would be able to easily venture out and explore other ways of life. This is the a chew the meat and spit out the bones style of living. However its time to update that principle by being more reserved and observing environments to peel the banana and eat the fruit. Let's go vegan!

Removal vs Remodel

Lets take a look at the decision of removing things from our lives or remodeling our lives in a way that is more conducive to our lives. Every scenario that is described as negative isn't worth removing. For instance, the big brother that often gets into fights and trouble often gets put to use by his younger and less aggressive sibling. Why is this? If the younger sibling is living a lifestyle that isn't troublesome and is overall positive, why wouldn't they choose to totally remove this older sibling from their lives? Well, despite the fact that it is harder to remove a family member from your life, it's actually better to remodel your life and keep them in their proper place. Before you say to yourselves "wait a minute this is considered using people", it's important to understand that their is nothing wrong with using people. The problem lies with misusing people and in fact if you can't be used that may in effect render you useless. This is where remodeling comes into play. We have to be able place every thing, person and scenario in its proper place within our lives. When we understand balance we see that their exist polarities in everything even though some things have an overall charge. If we choose to simply remove everything due to one side of its polarity we can end up in a state of emptiness.

When there exist things that attack us at the core they should be immediately removed from our circumference. This doesn't mean that we always have to remove the object, person or scenario. Sometimes we have to actually remove ourselves. This is easier to do because this is where the greatest amount of control lies, with ourselves. We not only posses greater control over our own lives than we do over the things that happen around us, but we have a greater responsibility to control the happenings in our own lives than what happens around us. Making our own lives truly better for us make the world around us better to live in. It's important to be honest about the true meaning of better. We may look at someone who is extremely successful and think to ourselves, "what have they done for anyone else?" At this point we are completely ignoring the visual of success that they've provided for us. By now we should understand that everything in life is not physical and the energy transference between us on this planet is in many cases much better than the instant gratification provided by a physical gift. Remember the practice of removing and remodeling our own homes is very similar the our lives. If we choose to say everything must go, what are we left with?

Pro vs Con

The pro vs con method of decision making has had a proven track record over the years and has become a staple in the way decisions are made amongst intelligent people. What many of us may not have noticed is that this is another example of balance because the method is actually completed by the use of the scale. When things become unbalanced the scale tips and the decision is rendered. If we choose to go against the decision rendered by the scale then we are simply going against the odds in hopes that things will go in our favor. Sometimes in life we do have to gamble. Every choice we make can not solely rely on the use of the scales, we have to factor in the gut feeling that in some cases can rule out all others. However, understanding the nature of polarity I think its best to take a different look at the concept of pro vs con. Things are inherently negative can yield positive outcomes and in the same regard the opposite can also occur. What we have to do is be able to weigh this negativity against the outcome. This is what's known as collateral damage. No one is going to achieve success without accepting some level of collateral damage. The way we asses this damage relies on our moral composition. Our climb to the top doesn't have to consist on stepping the heads of others in order to do so. The most dangerous way this effects our being is when we begin to step on parts of ourselves in order to enhance another part of our being, but it is a necessary factor in the way that we get further in life. In order to properly make decisions we must acknowledge the damage it will cause equally to the success that we are looking for. There are parts of our being that we are willing to sacrifice and parts of us that will be a refined unbeknownst to our present state of mind. We should use any available time to reflect on the decisions that we make in order to live comfortably with them. This is where the phrase "would you kill the world to save yourself" is most applicable because it applies to someone who didn't properly asses the outcome of choice that was made.

With the understanding of weighing things evenly to reach a positive outcome, there is also the existence of the gut feeling. However, what a lot of people don't realize is the gut feeling actually stems from the previous decisions we've made in our lives. If we've consistently made the choice to make negative decisions we've calibrated ourselves toward negative energy and our gut feeling will now also become geared toward negativity. This is the nature of a loser and if we wish to be winners in life we have to acknowledge the existence of losers because this is what balance is. If the gut feeling of positivity didn't exist there would be no lottery winners in the history of the world because if properly weighed on the scales the decision to buy a lotto ticket would obviously be out weighed by the probability of losing. However, the gut feeling can override logic in weighs that can be extremely profitable for us as individuals. Learning how to weigh our choices in life is a process that happens over time and is unique to the situations that we apply them to but greatly effects the overall charge of our being. It's very similar to the way that our bodies process food. Foods that aren't good for us are stored in our gut due to the way that our bodies process them and the foods that reach the gut are a direct result of the choice we made to eat them. So in essence, in order to trust our gut we have to make responsible decisions in order to have a gut worth trusting.

Influence or Irritants

Are you influenced by what irritates you? Are you irritated by what influences you? These questions can be easily answered with the right amount of introspection. Think about what motivates you and asses how it makes you feel internally. Some of us are motivated by what we don't particularly subscribe to, but this isn't necessarily a bad thing. Sometimes negativity promotes positivity. We can be fueled by what we do not want to become. If you are this type of person you have to be careless not to become consumed by the negativity that you focus on. What happens all to often in this scenario is we forget to recognize the good in what we've become in the process of focusing on what we disdain. It's as simple as looking to become successful rather than looking to not become unsuccessful. It sounds like the same thing because both outcomes equal success. However, the roads traveled to achieve this outcome are very different and can effect our levels of success very differently as well. When we look to what we don't want to be for inspiration we are being influenced by our irritants. This process can make the road to our success a more grueling one because people that are truly driven will constantly look for motivation to achieve success. This places us in search of the negativity that we are looking to not become. Rather than walking down the street and ignoring what you don't want to become we become attracted to it to fuel our ambition and remind us of what we don't want to become at the same time reminding us what we do want to become.

What's the difference between these two different approaches of achieving the success that we are looking for in life? Happiness. Placing more focus on what we want to become allows us to consume more positive images and subsequently more positive energy. This also allows you to properly acknowledge the success that you have while seeking a greater level of success. In mathematics this is called either rounding up to the highest common denominator or rounding down to the lowest common denominator.

The key to both of these scenarios is to enjoy what you have, while in search of greater to avoid the syndrome of never enough. When you focus on negativity you will not be able able to enjoy what you do have without wondering why you're in such close proximity to what you deem as negativity. Adversely, focusing on high levels of success often disable our ability to appreciate the success that we've already achieved. What's the answer for this? Be thankful! Take the time to be thankful for what exists around us as well as our own existence. We have to be just as thankful for the journey toward success as we are for the actual success. Being thankful for the influences and in some cases the irritants places us in the positive state that all humans are in search of and is the final key to the calibration of our being. With that being said before we reach the final section of this publication I'd like to thank you the reader for making it this far and I truly hope it serves you well. I'm taking the time to thank you now because at this moment it is the appropriate gesture. Even though we haven't reached the end of this quite yet its just as important to be thankful while on the journey as it is to be thankful at the end of it.

Completion
The Circle: The End is the Beginning

Well, here we are, not at the end but at the beginning of a new journey. If you've attempted to apply even a few of the principles in this book its not only appropriate for me to congratulate you, but you should be congratulating yourself as well. You've embarked on a journey within traveling to your very core similar to the rings that exist inside of a tree. Had the tree never been cut down we not have known these rings existed, yet whether the cut down or not they would have still existed. There are aspects of our core that at this stage of our being will remain a mystery, but its the work that we've committed to understanding what we do know of ourselves that makes unlocking these mysteries all the more possible. Don't fool yourselves into thinking the exercises in this book were an easy feet. You've unlocked parts of yourself that will never be fully locked away again and have crafted a better you, fully equipped to handle the calibration of yourself as well as aid in the calibration of others and for this you should be commended.

Remember, practice may not make you perfect but it will certainly make you better. Creating a better you is what changes the world for the better. However, this process is in no way void of mistakes. They are simply a part of this process and journey and should be accepted for what they are. Remember the polarities that exist around you, especially in regards to the mistakes that are made. Although they may be a hindrance and in some instances derail us temporarily, these mistakes are more than the learning experiences they are chalked up as. They are a part of the experiences we are blessed to have prior to receiving the breath of life and for that alone we should be grateful. Continuing to make mistakes is continuing to live and continuing your practice is continuing to grow.

In the most appropriate way to come full circle, we've now begun the three hundred and sixtieth paragraph of this book, bringing it to its completion. However, arriving at the end is also arriving at a new beginning. This new beginning is not what's common referred to as a clean slate. It's actual a restructured and reorganized slate that is more powerful than a blank one void of energy. This is a slate built of all of your life experience organized by a fresh new outlook and perspective on where you are and where your headed. With this, I thank you the reader and am confident in the abilities that you posses to make your lives better, making the world we live in a better place for us all.

"Enjoy Life" - Jus One

.

www.ingramcontent.com/pod-product-compliance
Lightning Source LLC
Chambersburg PA
CBHW071537040426
42452CB00008B/1049